else may never read it again
answer —

It keeps me from getting
flat, so I can recall
brighter side of life to
lonesome blokes at Padre
Hour. Some times they
see only mud & roof line
& sweat & damp cloths
in the morn & tasteless
meals & moneyless pockets
— no Second Front &
no chance of promotion.
Our Bed roll weight
is limited so I couldn't
bring Gramaphone &
Mc Cormack, Kreisler &
Paderewski all of whom I
heard personally in Detroit
Very well! we'll compose
our own. Lets go lads.
out pipe the Pipers.

THE PADRE'S WAR DIARY

Published by Brian Dalton

Text and reproductions of artwork
Copyright 2016 © by Brian Dalton

ISBN: 978-0-9947665-1-9

First Edition September 2016
  2 3 4 5 6 7 8 9 10

Printed in Canada by: Progressive Results Group, Kincardine

1. Biography, Diary
2. Canadian Forces WW II
3. Chaplains Corps
4. Post Traumatic Stress Disorder

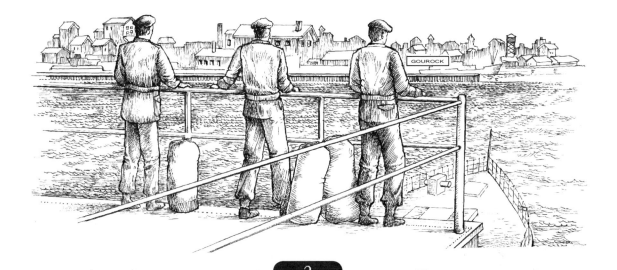

The Royal Canadian Army
Chaplain Corps
Cap Badge

DESCRIPTION

Superimposed upon a wreath of oak-leaves and laurels,
a Maltese cross. On the centre of the cross an annulus
inscribed "IN THIS SIGN CONQUER"; within the annulus
a quatrefoil voided; the whole surmounted by the Crown.

Rev. Major 'Mike' Dalton

Brian Dalton
2016

For my Dad

*Sometime in the mid 1950's when my family had
no television and needed groceries more than books,
my father brought home a set of books with the
strange name of encyclopedias. They were printed
in black and white with line drawing illustrations.*

*Among the many worlds that man did not
receive from nature but created out of his
own mind, the world of books is the greatest.
Without the word, without the writing of
books, there is no history, there is no
concept of humanity.*

*We need not fear a future elimination of the
book. On the contrary, the more that certain
needs for entertainment and education are
satisfied through other inventions, the more
the book will win back in dignity and
authority.*

*Hermann Hesse (July 2, 1877–Aug 9 1962)
from a 1930 essay titled "The Magic of the Book"
published in My Belief: Essays on Life and Art.*

FOREWORD

It is unlikely that the author of this diary, Major Rev. Mike Dalton ever intended for it to be illustrated. In a strange way it had to be written twice.

What started as a minor interest in a stored trunk of diaries, letters, old photographs, old books with many notes scribbled in the margins, medals and other ephemera, has grown into honoring an uncle's war time experiences.

Once the diarist's 'Padre' Mike Dalton's medals were mounted the incentive to do something with his diary took place. A rough time line of the diary entries was organized. This was compared to historical dates and events. At this point anyone could have been excused if it had been put back into the trunk and considered a passing fancy.

Brian Dalton didn't do that. His humble respect would see this project through. A retired visual Art teacher in Wellington County and an accomplished artist, Brian is a son of Huron County who remembers his childhood roots. His idea of an illustrated diary is uncommon. Like it's Graphic Novel cousin, it adds clarity to the story. It strings some of the diary together in a way some might otherwise find choppy.

It has taken Brian over 4½ years and 200 illustrations to finish this project. During this time I have been glad to be of assistance in his getting an education in the art of military form. Many changes had to be made from initial sketches."When did the allies start using that particular tank?", "How was the cockpit of that plane laid out?","What was the inscription on the Victoria Cross that was awarded to Mike's altar boy Fred Tilston?" Then came the abbreviations, of which some were official, while others Mike made up. This translation was slow.

The whole process lead to meetings, some planned, some made up on the spot and some with knowledgeable strangers offering good advice. But finally the end came. With the last selection and editing of a diary entry, and the last of the drawings revised, all that was left was the demobilization of the artist.

The War Diary is unique. Both times it was written was an adventure and both equally important.

Tim Wellstead

*Tim Wellstead is the owner of Condor Fine Books in Kincardine
and the Book Barn, Wingham.
He is a member of the OMRS Orders and Medals Research Society,
the RCMI Royal Canadian Military Institute,
and the CSMMI Canadian Society of Military Medals and Insignia.*

ACKNOWLEDGMENTS

In the years of this project I received much help from my wife Ruth, who endured being a proof reader and viewer for the 200 drawings I struggled with as I completed them, or 'thought' I had completed them.

My sons and daughters-in-law gave their thoughts and looked things over for me. Mary Jane especially provided me with appreciated close readings and Sheila gave good advice regarding layout. My granddaughter Jasmin was a big help in digitizing all my selected handwritten diary entries and saving them for me in a format that I could use. She also set up the fund raising site and assured me that this project has value.

My thanks to Kevin Newman, who served as my model for the images of a young Mike in Part One. Throughout the past 5 years I received valuable insights and financial support from my cousin Pat O'Connor. One of the Padre's nieces, Pat is a daughter of the Padre's sister Margaret and a sister of the pilot George, (in the diary) whose plane went down in the North Sea. She was present in March 1946 at the train station in Toronto when the Padre returned to Canada.

In the early days of this project my ex-partner in teaching, Monika Lassner made interesting and imaginative suggestions. Tim Wellstead owner of Condor Fine Books in Kincardine has been an invaluable guide. His loan of numerous books and his knowledge of military history and such things as WW 2 medals and equipment has been invaluable, as has been his unflagging encouragement. Two Art College colleagues, Al Holley and Dave Alexander, were good enough to look over my early efforts. Irv Mills, printer and designer (now retired), was essential to my getting things ready to print in this and other projects. Shell McConville a unique thinker and writer, helped with Mike's more obscure quotations. Wesley Bates, Artist and Wood Engraver, gave me some excellent observations keeping me focused on paying attention to design and drawing. Robert McEachern, historian and teacher, provided information and motivated through the example of his own work.

Leonard MacAulay, Sgt. Rtd. Royal Canadian Electro-mechanical Engineers, as a vet of more recent conflicts, made some very helpful observations.

The staff of the Owen Sound & North Grey Union Public Library, has always been forthcoming, helping me find books and information. Special thanks to Carolin Brooks. Many thanks to Gloria Williams for a final proof reading. Any mistakes that remain are my own.

My very special thanks to those generous relatives, friends, acquaintances and people I have not met for their financial support. Without their donations this book would not exist. It also seems important to mention my use of Google. The material acquired through Google made my research much simpler.

INTRODUCTION

The purpose of this introduction is to clarify the structure of the book and help the reader understand the book's arrangement.

The book's main body is in Part Three—'The Diary Years'. The material in Part Three is taken from a typed transcript of my uncle Michael Dalton's WW 2 War Diary which was originally published in photocopy form. It included his diary entries made during WW 2, and material he added later. He made diary entries from March 1942 to March 1946. Selected entries are taken verbatim from his originals. A few typos and name place spellings are corrected. Some material has been added from his 'Diary Supplement', which was written in 1976 during a tour he made of the same countries in which he traveled with his beloved Essex Scottish Regiment 30 years earlier.

This book's end sheets are copies of pages from the only one of many, small, black books that remains. He carried those with him and against Army regulations, kept his personal War Diary. He also kept an official officer's diary.

Part One-'The Early Years' starts with an actual event that happened when Mike was 11 years old. My father Dennis, Mike's youngest brother, often spoke of the Great Lakes Storm of 1913 and the loss of 250 men and 19 ships. He talked about how he and Mike, against their parents' wishes, watched drowned men's bodies being put into horse drawn wagons on the shore of Lake Huron near their home.

I am making what I think is a reasonable assumption that the event could have been as memorable and significant to Mike as it was to my father and may been a factor in Michael's future.

The 'Early Years' includes material from my father's reminiscences and my own imagined idea of what a precocious young Catholic boy in 1913, may have spoken about with a parish priest after having the traumatic experience of seeing dead bodies up close. This theme is picked up again in Part Three when Mike, now a Padre, listens to others who have been through the trauma of war.

Luckily the Padre's 'Apologia Pro Vita Sua' has survived and is included to provide background to Mike's early years. The family photographs taken 18 years apart, provide a sense of the environment and times Mike was born into.

Part Two—The 'War Years Before the Diary' is based on material Mike wrote before, after and during the War. This part is a brief look at some of the experiences Mike had from the time he volunteered in September 1939, to March 1942, when, after over 2 years in uniform, he decided to start his personal diary.

Throughout Part Three I have created one sided conversations in which a soldier speaks with the Padre in conversations or during the Catholic ritual of Confession. These are included at times in the diary when the Padre mentions 'hearing Confessions'. Some of the soldier's reports are included to describe aspects of stress, fear and anxiety a soldier experienced that often lead to what was then called 'Battle Fatigue' or 'Shell Shock', now called Post Traumatic Stress Disorder.

Decades later Mike spoke of soldiers' fears and anxiety, remembering them calling out for their mothers or "crying like babies" (an expression he used matter-of-factly, with compassion, not with condescension or sarcasm). In the Confessions, or conversations, a soldier's verbal description of a stressful experience during action enabled me to include an illustration of an event or battle the Padre mentions in the diary but may not have witnessed first hand.

The *editor's notes* are intended to provide some information that I'm sure the Padre would approve of. Sometimes they are included when the Padre's terms or references may be obscure. Referring to his sister Margaret, Mike alternated between spelling her name with and without the letter 't'. Margaret's family pronounced her name as "Margarie".

His love of music, Shakespeare and English poetry and his good memory for quotations is obvious throughout. I have left some imperfect quotations- made in semi darkness by candle light, they are forgivable. It should also be remembered to read the entries in the context of a 'diary', which typically employs a kind of language short form. After reading a few pages, it should be obvious that the Padre left out the definite article 'the' sometimes and used it at other times.

Some of Mike's phrases and 'sayings' and playing with words may sound quite archaic after 77 years, but that is what makes his writing authentic. His love of sport drew him to use a baseball metaphor when describing a battle or raid ("no hits, no runs etc.").

The lists of names at the end of the book is necessary. It is a reminder that these men of Mike's Regiment are only a few of the thousands who:

> "lived, felt dawn, saw sunset glow, loved and were loved".
> Lieutenant Colonel John McCrae

As mankind seems to be stumbling awkwardly towards a world without war, it is my hope that The Padre's Diary can contribute something to a realization of just how horrible war in any era is. In spite of the evils that exist it is worth remembering the words of the Padre's favorite Englishman.

> "What a piece of work is a man! How noble in reason,.."
> Shakespeare Hamlet.

Tennyson's Monument

EDITOR'S / ILLUSTRATOR'S NOTES

The initial motivation for deciding to illustrate my uncle's war diary went through some significant changes. Initially I thought I would simply take a few diary highlights and draw some illustrations to accompany them. The original photocopied diary has been around for over half a century. The padre had 1000 copies printed originally and another 1000 printed in 1967 which he claimed to have mailed all over Canada. I knew few people who could claim that they actually had read the entire thing. It was not an easy document to read. It was cluttered with faded poorly photocopied photographs. These were the source of some illustrations. I tried reading it as a child and then in my 20's, but set it aside. Reading it again as I became a senior, I realized what an amazing personal record of war it is. My father had always praised his brother's diary and I finally came to see why. Now of course, I wish I had started the project while my father and uncle were still alive.

My motivation was never to pay homage to only the Padre, but also to those thousands of men and women who volunteered and lost their lives in WW 2.

The Padre was a complex mix of a socially minded priest who adhered to church doctrines in only some ways. As a non-conforming rebel he liked the idea of a senior officer who compared him with Michael the Archangel, the biblical figure who is usually depicted as a protector with a sword. However his diary has far more quotes taken from poetry and great men than from scripture. Those who knew him said that like Churchill, he felt he was beyond injury. He used to say that in his 6 war years he "couldn't even catch a cold". It seems his above average physical stamina accounted for his good fortune. Even into late middle age he could swim long distances and true to his nature to show off, as a youth he actually swam across the Detroit River. On sports days during the war, in cross country runs, he easily outdid most of the men who were half his age.

As a Catholic Priest he knew all the rituals but said: "the war changed all that". He became an advocate of Ecumenism (the aim of promoting unity in all the world's Christian churches). In the diary he makes a point to praise the men in his many contacts who weren't Catholic. It is also revealing of his attitude to note his diary dedication: "I dedicate this Diary to Total War to all those Jews and non Catholics who helped make my war years livable and I hope useful".

225 diary entries were originally chosen to give what I thought was an overall and reasonable sense of the entire diary. The number grew to 329 entries selected from the total of 528 that the Padre made in his last 4 years of service.

During the years of this project from 2011 to 2016, my motivation altered. I became aware of the many disturbing reports of the consequences of Post Traumatic Stress Disorder in the military and elsewhere. As I worked I realized I had the opportunity to use my diary project to contribute to what seemed like a growing awareness of the results of the condition. That realization motivated me to include the soldiers' Confessions and conversations with the Padre.

I was born a year after the Padre came home in 1946. Thus, for most of the first decade after the war I was too young to recognize his condition of somewhat hyperactive and erratic behavior which older people have told me about.

In my large family there were various opinions and feelings about that character we called "Father Mike". No one ever called him Father Michael. My father admired him and my mother was quick to point out his "too human" flaws. In a moment of weakness however, she called him the most handsome man she ever saw.

My own relationship with the uncle was all fun all the time. We had a lot in common. We were born in the same community of Kingsbridge and swam and fished in the same Lake Huron. We both traveled to the lake on the same trail and had similar childhood traumatic experiences there. We both attended the same country school. He attended University and a Seminary and became a priest. I attended Art College and Universities and became a teacher. Around his 102nd birthday I told him that I had a wife, two sons and 2 grand children (now 5). He claimed to have had over 500 men of war who called him 'Father'. I told him I had maybe 1000 students who called me 'sir' (among other things). He said he sent home over 1000 letters to next of Kin. I replied that I sent home almost that many report cards. He claimed he could play any instrument badly, I admitted to just one. However there was one time when he revealed that he didn't know much about children as he almost cruelly teased my young son Dennis beyond the normal boundaries of teasing.

Otherwise he was always a source of fun and encouragement as he tried to teach me how to swim, or sat beside me on the piano bench, listening or playing what he called his goofy songs. Twice he even purchased artwork from me. On one very memorable occasion, when I spent a summer in 1962 as an Army cadet at Camp Ipperwash, he visited me with another uncle Ray. When I gave them a camp tour the Padre seemed uncharacteristically quiet. Standing beside my bunk he seemed to be inspecting the entire barracks. He walked out onto the vast Battalion parade square into the hot empty space and just stood there. At the time as a 15 year old I noticed his uncharacteristic mood but wasn't insightful enough to understand.

Now I can imagine how he must have been recalling those war years with his "lads", many of whom died at Dieppe only 20 years earlier in that same month of August. Many were only a few years older than I was then. Reading the diary and research material on PTSD I came to realize at a deeper level just how destructive war is and how the Padre meant it literally when he said: "War is hell."

Part One

A childhood Episode
foreshadowing the Padre's future.

Mike's family in 1914.

Back row: Walter, John S., 'Himself' (Mike aged 12).
Center row: Margaret, Morgan, Fr.McCormack, Mary, Josie.
Front row: Dennis, Helen, Antoinette, Raymond.
Deceased as children: Uriel, Monica.

Michael is the 5th child in a family of 11. Nine children survived.
He is the son of Mary Sullivan and Morgan Dalton. Michael's
grandfather Maurice Dalton immigrated from Ireland in 1841.

Editor's note   *This photograph was taken on the occasion of Mike's
parents Mary and Morgan's 25th Wedding Anniversary.*

November 1913
St. Joseph's Church Kingsbridge, Ashfield Township, Huron County, Province of Ontario, Dominion of Canada

It has been one week since the great storm of 1913. It was called the White Hurricane and raged from November 7 to 10. Heavy snowfalls and high winds devastated the Great Lakes. Nineteen ships were lost and the same number stranded. Two hundred and fifty sailors died, many in Lake Huron. One ship, the Carruthers, went down in the area of Lake Huron north of Kingsbridge.

Eleven year old Michael Joseph Dalton makes his way with a heavy heart through deep snow from the recent storm to St. Joseph's, the new Roman Catholic church in Kingsbridge. The church was opened in 1905 and is less than a mile from Lake Huron.

Young Michael Dalton has been having a hard time with his conscience. After the big storm he and his little brother Dennis disobeyed their parents and walked to Lake Huron to see if there were any ship wrecks on the beach. In the tradition of his ancestors Michael is going to confess his disobedience to the parish priest Father Michael McCormick, after whom young Michael claims to have been named.

Bless me Father for I have sinned...I disobeyed my parents...They told me not to go to the lake, but we went anyway and I saw dead men being put into a wagon...

They were all banged up and I thought that someone should have been there to help them—maybe they were still alive ...now I can't stop wondering why God let them die.

When I go to bed I see the dead men's faces. It makes me feel really bad. I don't want to see them again. Is God punishing me for just looking? I was really angry at God, Is that bad?

If God loves us why does he let bad things happen? Sister Vincent says God loves us and his ways are a mystery but I still don't see why he has to let bad things like that storm happen.

No, God is not punishing you. You just saw something that no one of any age should see and I think it's normal to feel some anger.

Mike, we all wonder about those things. Your questions are ones that people have been asking for a very long time and it seems natural to me to wonder about such things.

One day later

After I went to confession I told my parents the truth... but now I can't stop thinking about what I saw at the beach...

Now I can't stop remembering the dead men's faces.

Mike we have to take
it on faith that God
knows what he is doing.
We should just be
honest and do the best
we can to help others.

Father, what do
you mean by
"take it on faith"?

When we say "take it
on faith", or "having
faith", it means we
trust that things will
turn out alright. When
we say: "your faith",
then we mean the
things you believe in.

I think I must have faith
then. I think everything
I do will turn out alright.
Even when we are losing
at hockey, I think we will
win. Sister Vincent says I
am an incurable optimist.
But I don't know about
that other kind of faith.

Being an optimist is
good! And in time
you will know about
that other kind
of faith.

But do you think
I will ever stop
thinking about
what I saw
at the lake ?

You may never forget what
you saw, but in time you will
see that it was one of those
tragedies that happen, and
that life is made up of both
good and bad. It is in the bad
times that the things you
believe in and your beliefs or
faith can help you be strong
and get through difficult
times, but now you should
go get ready for that hockey
game. Do you understand
the things I have said ?

I'm eleven years old.
I understand a lot.

Apologia Pro Vita Sua

*'Apologia pro vita sua'—a defense of one's life, or written
justification for one's beliefs or course of conduct.*

Written by Mike Dalton in an attempt to alert his cherished nieces
and nephews to the folly of falling behind in school.

I received the 8th grade prize in 1915 because my teacher had such a dumb entrance class that I had little opposition. She brought us to school a half hour early every day and half a day on Saturday. When Dad asked me to stay home and drive team on a gang plow I said: "Do you want me to be a farmer or a scholar?"

At that time I had no desire to be a priest. In 1916 my oldest sister said: "You'll only be an old bachelor if you stay on the farm". When I was fourteen my father drove me in his new Ford car to Goderich where I took the train to Assumption College in Windsor.

I lost a month in 2nd year school when I had the flu in 1918—the year the Allies beat the Germans. No one gave us a book to read to keep up in classes. Then by staying home for a month in 1919, I went from the frying pan into the fire. I never caught up. I failed a subject in 4th year High. In my first year in College I couldn't recover the loss, so I stayed out a year to farm, read, study and pray. With four hundred acres there was plenty of work.

It was 1925 when I went to Detroit to make Hudson cars. Room and board was ten dollars a week. Back at College in September 1925 I fell behind in Shakespeare. That was a blessing in disguise. I took this credit with the famous Mrs. Albright at the University of London. I have had an interest in Shakespeare and English poetry ever since and I can quote plenty of it. But time in her class was time I should have been in 3rd year University, so I fell behind in Latin and in 1927 I had two Latin classes to attend. One was over the lunch period. After the lights went out in the Seminary I continued to study in the bathroom. With one small supplement in Chaucer I finally caught up to a B. A. in 1928 and ordination from St. Peter's Seminary by Bishop O'Connor in 1932.

In an inscrutable design of Divine Providence in the same year, my first funeral Mass was for my mother Mary. I celebrated my very first Mass in Kingsbridge, where I grew up. My first years as a parish priest were in Windsor Ontario at Holy Name of Mary Church and later at St. Alphonsus. My first funeral Mass in uniform was for my father Morgan.

Goderich 14 miles

Mike's family in 1932

This family photograph was taken shortly
after Mike's Ordination, and his first Mass
in his family church in Kingsbridge Ontario.

Left to right
Back row: Antoinette, Dennis, Raymond, Walter, Josie, John S., Margaret.
Front row: Mary, Helen (Sister Maureen), Father Mike, Morgan.

Part Two
The War Years Before the Diary
September 1939 – March 1942

Part two consists of material taken from the Padre's archives. It covers the time from his volunteering in September 1939 to his arrival in England in July 1940. He did not start his Personal War Diary in England until 2 ½ years later in March 1942. One of the few times he mentions the conditions in England before the diary, is included here by way of a letter to his brother Dennis' son, his newborn nephew Maurice Dalton. This period was during the Battle of the Atlantic and the Battle of Britain.

Editor's note— 'Captain' Father Mike trying the Bagpipes during training in Camp Borden Ontario.

LATE EDITION — Sept 1 1939

GERMANY INVADES POLAND

EXTRA — Sept 3 1939

BRITAIN AND FRANCE DECLARE WAR

WAR DECLARED

EXTRA **The London Free Press** EXTRA

London Ontario's foremost newspaper
London City and Sunday, September 1, 1939

THREE CENTS   THREE CENTS

CANADA IS NOW AT WAR

September 1 1939

Your Excellency,

If you are called upon to furnish Chaplains for the service I shall be ready on land sea or air.

Yours in Christ
Mike Dalton

Proclamation of War

OTTAWA, Sept. 10 (CP).—Following is the text of the proclamation published today in an extra edition of the Canada Gazette declaring a state of war exists between Canada and Germany:

TWEEDSMUIR,
(L.S.),
CANADA:

George the Sixth, by the Grace of God, of Great Britain, Ireland and the British Dominions beyond the Seas, King, Defender of the Faith, Emperor of India.

To all to whom these presents shall come or whom the same may in anywise concern,

Greeting:

A PROCLAMATION.
ERNEST LAPOINTE, ATTORNEY-GENERAL, CANADA.

Whereas by and with the advice of our Privy Council for Canada we have signified [ou]r approval of the issue of a proclamation [in] the Canada Gazette declaring that a state [of] war with the German Reich exists and [h]as existed in our Dominion of Canada as [a]nd from the 10th day of September, 1939:

Now therefore we do hereby declare [and] proclaim that a state of war with the [Germ]an Reich exists and has existed in our [Domin]ion of Canada as from the 10th day of [Septem]ber, 1939.

[O]f all which our loving subjects and [oth]ers whom these presents may con[ce]rn hereby required to take notice and [govern] themselves accordingly.

[In] testimony whereof we have caused [o]ur letters to be made patent and the [Great] Seal of Canada to be hereunto affixed. [Witnes]s: Our right trusty and well-beloved [John] Baron Tweedsmuir of Elsfield, a mem[ber of] our most honorable Privy Council, [Knight] Grand Cross of our most distinguished [Order] of Saint Michael and Saint George, [Knight] Grand Cross of our Royal Victorian [Order,] member of our Order of the Compan[ions of] Honor, Governor-General and Com[mande]r-in-Chief of our Dominion of Canada.

[At] our Government House, in our City [of Ott]awa, this 10th day of September, in [the ye]ar of Our Lord One Thousand Nine [Hundr]ed and Thirty-Nine and in the third [year of] our Reign.

By Command,

[W.] L. MACKENZIE KING,

Louis Bergeron -Batman to Rev. Captain Mike Dalton

Louis volunteered to be my Batman, secretary, typist, chauffeur, carpenter, jeep driver, laundry man, Mass server, and Aide de Camp. Louis never swore or stole our cigarettes, or drank our rum ration. Louis erected our suitcase 'Collapsible Cathedral' on the windswept sands of Camp Borden, in the stately Isle de France and from camp to camp in England and Europe. Louis was to save my life near Caen in France by insisting one night that he take our truck back for repairs. That meant that I had to sleep under ground. Shrapnel hit everything that night in the trees where the truck would have been. In the morning I crawled out of the trench to find my helmet pierced with shrapnel. I got down on my knees and thanked God I wasn't in it—thanked Louis too.

I like life in the Barracks. The precision of the Army is marvelous, so are the officers. Our Regiment minister quoted Pius XI in an address to officers. We get along like two peas in a pod, the same pod.

From a letter to the Padre's niece Marguerite—January 1940

Spring 1940 Camp Borden Ontario

Padres of the Essex Scottish testing their ability at some carpentry as they construct a bed at Camp Borden. At left is Capt. the Rev. C. W. Cline, Protestant, with Capt. the Rev. M. J. Dalton, Catholic.

June 1 1940–Captain Mike Dalton

*Editor's note   Mike Dalton's war years were initially with the **Essex Scottish Regiment** which was created in 1885 and joined with the Kent Regiment in 1954 to become* **The Essex and Kent Scottish Regiment.**

In June 1940 Mike was appointed Chaplain of the 4th Brigade including the:

Essex Scottish

Hamilton Light Infantry

Royal Canadian Regiment

Regimental Marches:
The Highland Laddie
& A Hundred Pipers.
Motto: Semper Paratus
(Always Ready)

Regimental Marches:
Mountain Rose
Motto: Semper Paratus
(Always Ready)

Regimental Marches:
St. Catherines
&Pro Patria
Motto: Pro Patria
(For Country)

Captain Mike insisted on being involved in all aspects of a soldier's training. Here, during the training months in Canada, he is receiving instruction in the use of the army's Lee Enfield rifle.
Although he steadfastly refused to wear the recommended side arm, he proved himself an expert shot. He said it came from hunting rabbits on his father's farm. In his notes he boasts: "4 Bulls out of 5".

JUNE 18 1940 France has fallen. We are alone and you are in here when you should be out there with the others, muscling up for the job you have taken on. You're soldiers whether you like it or not, and you must learn to carry yourselves as soldiers out there with your fellow men.

Editor's note
The Windsor Star reports the Padre's speaking to men in a detention center. One month later the Star reports as the Regiment embarks from Halifax for England on the Empress of Australia with the escort H.M.S. Revenge.

Empress of Australia

En route, there was an air of anticipation. The new Army Chaplain's thoughts were not too far off the rest of his lads. He could understand and enjoy the adventure and romance that a regiment of one thousand young men around 20 were feeling. They were feeling optimistic that their arrival would end the war. As the 2nd Canadian Division, they were the only fully equipped Division that could travel on wheels in England. England's equipment was at Dunkirk in France.

JULY 30 1940 To the voyager land is always a welcome sight, and at Gourock near Glasgow I join the sergeants, men and officers in singing:

I Belong to Glasgow

I belong to Glasgow

But when I get a couple of drinks on a Saturday Glasgow belongs to me.

I presume that everyone knows that non-Catholic Chaplains were servicing their Regiments in their way spiritually, socially etc. Their acceptance by all is evident by the fact that all Regiments of our fourth Brigade had Chaplains decorated by the King for spiritual and physical courage. These men were:

Major Rev. John Foote–   V.C.   R.H.L.I.
Major Rev. Harold Appleyard– M.C. R.Reg.C.
Major Rev. Joe Cardy–   M.C. Essex Scottish

An ecumenical spirit was unavoidable and natural. To meet our lads, I had to mingle with thousands of non-Catholics—had to sit on my cot to read my Breviary prayers, while they were reverently silent. We buried their men, they ours, as bleak occasion demanded. We instructed those of our own faith for marriage etc. At times when no rabbi was available I instructed a few Jews on the only marriage doctrine I know. The Colonel made the final decision—to marry or not.

1940–41
Count John McCormack

The famous Irish tenor often sang for the soldiers. I heard him in concerts and was at his estate four times. I visited his grave in Ireland in 1945. He died at 61 years of age. Oh John...

Dear Father Dalton, Thanks and God love you for Yours, grand kind letter It warmed the cockles of my heart am feeling fine Just had a bit of a chill your friend John McCormack Aug 15 1941

Requiescat in Pacem—*Rest in Peace*

Excerpt from Mike's letter to his nephew Maurice Dalton

Editor's note *The Padre estimated that he sent over 1000 letters to Next of Kin. He also wrote many letters to family members. This excerpt from a letter to his brother Dennis' five week old son Maurice was written after arriving in England and is included here to reveal some of the conditions in England before Mike started his diary 10 months later.*

Dear Maurice,   12 May 1941

   Little man I am privileged to pen these lines, from the front lines of the last citadel of freedom as we know it. I visited London the morning after one of the heaviest air raids on the Red Lion, the Heart of the Empire. I walked amidst charred ruins of historic marble and stone edifices. Hundreds of firemen were plying their hoses in high crevices in the walls.

   We frequently brushed off the burning embers from our shoulders, as they were driven out by force of the water. I asked a fireman if anyone might still be living in the ruins. Propping one foot on the preserved mummy of a crusader of past centuries, and lighting one of my Canadian cigarettes on a glowing ember of the Temple Round Church off Fleet Street, he replied: "God only knows".

> *"Beneath the smouldering ruins*
> *perhaps are laid*
> *some hearts once pregnant with celestial fire.*
> *Hands that the rod of Empire might*   *-Thomas Gray*
> *have swayed*   *Elegy written in a*
> *or walked to ecstasy the living lyre".*   *Country Churchyard*

   After my Mass for 4th Brigade I rushed to Westminister Cathedral to stand among seven hundred French in exile at solemn high Mass in honor of Joan d' Arc. The smoke of burning London in our nostrils, we thrilled to the organ bellowing Marseilles."Aux armes les citoyens, formez vos bataillons".

> *"Breathes there a man so dead*
> *that never to himself hath said*   *-Sir Walter Scott*
> *This is my own, my native land !"*   *Breathes there the Man*

   Right in church rifles were shouldered as de Gaulle, Free French Forces, Army, Air and Navy marched out with obstinate determination in their faces. Many eyes were bedewed on the faces of madams and mademoiselles.

   I am charged to a deeply conscious responsible extent with the murmuring of Christian virtues in five hundred gallant and loyal 4th Brigadiers in order that we may be worthy to keep vigilant guard on the front lines of freedom. Although smoke of burning London may be in our nostrils, the discordant din of A.A. fire in our ears, and the pathetic sight of the soldier bidding fond adieu to wife and kiddies before our eyes, yet in our inner senses we feel that God is still in the heavens.

   We are here to defend the principle that you can eat praties with their jackets on or consume rice out of a washtub as the spirit moves you. We are here to defend the principle that you may kneel opposite the 11th station in St Joseph's Church or worship toads in McCarn's creek. Little man, we who are prepared to die if necessary to defend these principles that you may have a fuller life, salute you from the front citadel of freedom.

        Cheerio
        Uncle Mike

Part Three – The Diary Years
March 1942 – March 1946

From September 1939, when Father Mike wrote his letter volunteering to be of service, through his time training in Canada and England, he kept an Official Officer's War Diary. In March 1942 against Military rules, the Padre made his first personal War Diary entry in a Diary he titled "Total War".
The first original small black diary book that he carried with him still exists. His complete diaries were typed in what must have been a monumental effort by Mrs. Lyons of Precious Blood Parish in Windsor. When all the diary material was assembled, the Padre, in his spirit of ecumenism, made the following dedication:

I dedicate this Diary "Total War" to all those Jews, non-Catholics and Catholics who helped to make my war years as liveable as possible and I hope useful.

Editor's note
Total War — is warfare that includes any and all civilian-associated resources and infrastructure as legitimate military targets, and justifies using weapons and tactics that result in significant civilian or other non-combatant casualties, whether collateral damage or not.

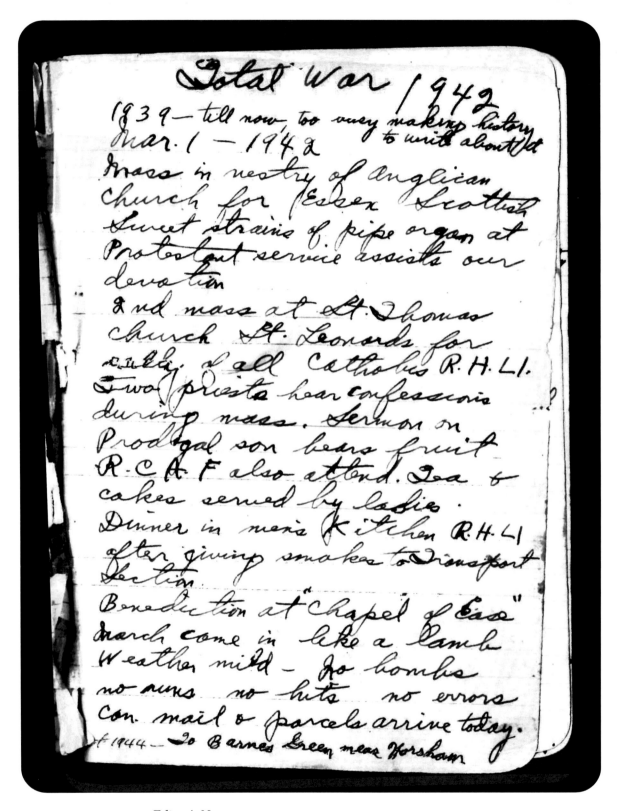

Total War 1942

1939 — till now, too busy making history to write about it

Mar. 1 — 1942

Mass in vestry of Anglican church for Essex Scottish. Sweet strains of pipe organ at Protestant service assists our devotion

2nd mass at St. Thomas church St. Leonards for entity of all Catholics R.H.L.I. Two priests hear confessions during mass. Sermon on Prodigal son bears fruit R.C.A.F also attend. Tea & cakes served by ladies.

Dinner in mens Kitchen R.H.LI after giving smokes to Transport Section

Benediction at "Chapel of Ease" March came in like a lamb Weather mild — No bombs no runs no hits no errors Con. mail & parcels arrive today.

+ 1944 — To Barnes Green near Horsham

Editor's Note
This is the first page of the original handwritten Diary covering the time from March 1942 until March 1946. It introduces the Padre's fondness for Baseball metaphors.

MAR 2 1942

Billeted in Grosvenor House. Roaring of Channel rocks us to sleep nightly. One mile away is where William the Conqueror, in 1066 made a successful invasion. This was the last time and it will be the last time due to the presence of Canada's gallant manhood.

MAR 9 1942

Answering mail by the roar of the Channel when suddenly windows shake violently-the siren hadn't sounded so it must be a sea battle. Concussion travels many miles-it reminded us of the days at Aldershot during the battle of Britain. It is good to hear these bombs, some never hear them and will never again hear with mortal ears.

> *"The boast of heraldry, the pomp of power,*
> *And all that beauty, all that wealth e'er gave,*
> *Awaits alike the inevitable hour.*
> *The paths of glory lead but to the grave."*

Thomas Gray
Elegy written in a
Country Churchyard

Gave H.Q. Company Lucky Strikes. American cigarettes are rare- so one to each. I have now given to men of Brigade over 50,000 cigarettes ($1,117.50) in Canadian money. These cigarettes are from friends in Windsor and elsewhere.

MAR 14 1942

First Battalion Parade under new O.C.Col. Jasperson. Breath of Spring in air. 4 o'clock incessant rumbling of guns! All rush to see two ships in the Channel. "C'est la guerre".

It's the War, (cannot be helped)

MAR 15 1942

Awakened at daylight by concussion which broke windows in our billets.

MAR 17 1942
St. Patrick's Day

Brigade scheme at Eastdean near Eastbourne. English sprinkling system at its best. All drenched. Trucks stalled in mud. Those who couldn't find barns stand in rain until dawn. (mock battle) C.Co. Essex Scottish have mock trial for Hitler—preceded by Irish songs. All enter in spirit of Great Feast, in spite of neutrality of Eire which many disapprove of. Three layers of rubber raincoat penetrated by rain. Sat in front seat of truck most of night. Too cold and wet to sleep. Thoughts took me back to Irish Concerts I attended in 1941.

MAR 23 1942

Attended lecture in White Rock Pavilion by Ian Hanna M.P.M.A. of Cambridge University Extension Lectures. Subject:"Lines of a Lasting Peace". He saw injustice of Versailles and recognizes culture of Germans. Revenge must be ruled out by the spirit of Christ.

APR 4 1942

Called to battle to talk to R.C.E.'s with marital troubles. Warrant came through from Brigade for trip to Eire.(It's not hard to take). First leave in seven months.

APR 6 1942

To Dublin—Easter Monday on leave. Irish Sea cantankerous.

    April 6 1940– Hitler spring offensive resulting in fall of France.
    April 9 1941– Hitler spring offensive resulting in fall of Yugoslavia and Greece.
    April 6 1942– Padre makes a bloodless invasion of Eire to renew spirit and faith
        and assist in resurrection of conquered races.

APR 12 1942
    Dublin is infested with jolly Irishmen- no black outs- lots to eat.

St. Pat's has high window donated by Guinness Brewery with inscription—Matthew XXV1

I WAS THIRSTY AND YOU GAVE ME DRINK

Last year's visit was from head to toe—Belfast, Cork, Kerry, and Cahirsiveen, home of my Grandpa Dalton who didn't want to eat up his old man's seed potatoes, so in 1841 left for Canada to be the first Deputy Reeve of Huron County—before Confederation.

MAY 18 1942

I give out thousands of cigarettes from friends in Windsor and elsewhere, giving a package for three or four men. One cigarette costs more than two cups of tea. 2,500 are worth $66.00 here. 900 warriors appreciate them.

Boarded boat at Portsmouth for Isle of Wight, landing and assault course. Marched seven miles to nearest station. Billeted with Protestant Chaplain Bob Patterson. Isle of Wight more beautiful than Eire—if possible—it isn't. Navy blokes working with us on barges which some day may barge into Europe have interesting stories of Norway and France. We often talk to R.A.F.

MAY 24 1942

Sunday mass in Lord Byron's old home. Military usually billet in castles of big shots since they are so spacious. At midnight Jerry puts on a show outside our bedroom. Planes fly over tree tops machine gunning and dropping bombs. I saw flashes of A.A. through window but didn't get up as many did. Blitzes are so common you can't see them all.(No hits, several runs, no hurts, plenty of moves).

Editor's note: After the war The Padre claimed he could sleep through anything

MAY 25 1942

Out with 'D' Company on M.C.L.'s—shooting from craft to target in Channel. Passed the castle where Queen Victoria died near Coves. Lads drenched with salt spray coming home. Queen Victoria said, "The sun never sets on the British Empire." The reason—because God couldn't trust them in the dark.

MAY 26 1942

Photographed with British soldier who shot down German plane with a Bren gun.

MAY 27 1942

Forced march by Battalion in fighting order. Some dropped out. I carried rifles or Tommy guns of those who weakened in 'D' Company of Major John Wills. When we tired marching we'd run a bit, distance 12 miles, usually a three hour jaunt. This time two hours 45 minutes. I am 40 years old this month, most men are in their 20's.

JUN 1 1942

12 mile route march in morning including mock battle on parachutists. I talked to old people who remembered Tennyson with cape, beard and smelly pipe.(his poetry doesn't smell, it stimulates). To his monument. He wrote 'Crossing the Bar' here.

Mike surely was thinking of the last stanza in which death is compared to crossing the "sandbar" between the tide or river of life, with it's outgoing "flood", and the sea that lies beyond death (boundless deep).

Comment by Shell McConville.

"For tho' from out our bourne of Time and Place
The flood may bear me far,
I hope to see my Pilot face to face
When I have crost the bar."

Tennyson
1809-1892

JUN 1 1942

A lad of A. Co. has too much beer and wants to shoot. A few bullets go astray till a Sergeant shoots him through the knee. He then surrendered his rifle. A court martial for him and possibly a lame knee.

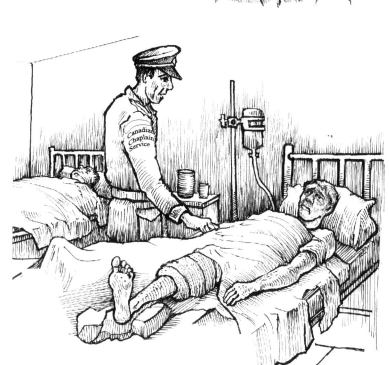

Padre, thanks for coming. I don't think I'll be here long—medics say my knee is too banged up for them to do anything. I might never bend it again. I'm being sent home as if I were some damned coward. Padre I'm so damned ashamed. I hardly remember—I was so drunk. I never thought I'd be one of those guys—we've both seen them, you know—fool. Yesterday a letter came telling me my mother died. Hell I didn't even know she was sick—and nobody was there with her. Yeah I know it's no excuse. I'll have a court martial I know that. I'll take what they give me, but how the hell will I ever tell anyone how I got shot? I can't see living with a lie, like I got it in action, or even in training.

Padre, you're an Officer people listen to you—tell the big shots we have to get doing something—something worthwhile. All the guys are sick of all this training... it seems for nothing.

JUN 3 1942

Heat of summer here, 1,000 bombers visit Germany. That's big business.

Editor's note– Actual number was 1036

JUN 11 1942

4th and 6th Bde. stage dawn practice attack on Bridgeport on mainland. Sea route for small craft. Many get sick. We left mother boat at two a.m. and were lowered into turbulent sea to travel 15 miles to objective. Big 40 ton tanks in landing scheme. Back wet and tired.

JUN 13 1942

Sports day—I am the only officer in the race finals—came in 3rd in Regiment Cross Country- of 3000 men in 4th Bde. only fourteen are faster. Colonel Pearson said I may be one of the 'Fallen Angels'—Michael—the Arch-Angel.

JUN 21 1942

Spent afternoon learning technique of Radio Field Sets- receiving and broadcasting. At request of Colonel all officers must be prepared to carry on if Signal Section falls.

JUN 22 1942

Reveille two a.m. Small boats lowered, one I was in carried our Brigadier Lett, a British General, an American Colonel and two Padres. Landing at Bridgeport at dawn and wading in. 40 ton tanks land. About 100 ships in flotilla took part in this 'invasion' of England.

JUL 2 1942

8000 troops, tanks, etc. embark for raid on France. I camouflaged my 'Collapsible Cathedral' to allay suspicion among men, as I brought it aboard. Secret was revealed by Colonel when embarked, so all could study maps for daylight raid. We were prepared for strong opposition, even Panzer troops might rush from Paris. Paratroops and 12 squadrons of R.A.F. would help. Mother ships would let down small craft about middle of English Channel. We would come back in A.L.C.'s. Confessions all afternoon, the greatest number since I joined the Army. B.H.Q. and C. Company were on Leopold ship, also Bde.H.Q.

The Essex Scottish
Cap Badge

DESCRIPTION

Two sprays of thistle supporting a scroll in the shape of
a pointed arch, bearing the designation "THE ESSEX
SCOTTISH"; across the thistles a scroll bearing the motto
"SEMPER PARATUS" (Always Ready); in the centre a shield
bearing in chief three seaxes barwise (alluding to the Arms
of the County Council of Essex); in base the White Horse
of Kent; the whole surmounted by a lion's head erased.

This was the Cap Badge during WW II.
Since then the name has been changed
to "THE ESSEX AND KENT SCOTTISH".

JUL 3 1942

10 p.m. Mass and Communion on eve of intended battle by special privilege. 100 went to Communion including a few Protestants. I didn't know until they told me later. There was never a Mass (at least in our experience), comparable to that Mass on the bow, of the ship with men standing amidst ropes, anchors etc.

JUL 3 1942

Somewhere on the Seven Seas we waited for favourable tide and wind till July 7. The elements were against us. Each morning I said Mass on board, almost all attended.

JUL 3 1942 Evening

In evening Brigadier Lett and Captain of the ship allowed me a special life boat to visit A and D Companies on the ship "Prince Charles". Confessions for two hours in gun turret on bow.

Bless me father for I have sinned. It has been years since my last confession, and I am sorry about that, but Padre I need your help. I don't know how to say it- I guess I'm just scared. I can't seem to stop thinking I'm going to get killed. It's all I've been thinking about Padre, I'm worried I can't stop....

I'm afraid I'll be a coward if we ever get into action. I get scared and shaky every time we have training with live ammo. I'm the worst shot in the platoon. Every loud noise makes me jump. I never used to be like this and I can't tell any of the other officers. In letters home I can't say anything about it.

Padre do you think we really are going on this raid? In a way I wish we would, maybe then I could get over this. I hope you don't have to tell anybody about this Padre, and Padre the guys really like the way you try to keep our spirits up. I don't know how you can be so damned energetic. Some of the guys say you never sleep.

JUL 4 1942

Party on board in honor of Americans in flotilla. Captain directs singing. We studied maps and photographs for a week. I was interested in learning all routes to R.A.P. and M.D.S. That was so I could meet wounded. I also sewed several hundred French Francs in my tunic, a steel file, a compass and a map of France and Germany in case taken prisoner and had a chance to escape. Also Iron rations for 24 hours were distributed.

JUL 6 1942

I had been caught in a few Blitzes so felt confident that the experience would help me to assist others. All wrote letters on board ship to be mailed if we did not come back. "Prayer of Drake" as he entered Cadiz in 1587 was given to all by Colonel Mann.

Disturb us, Lord when
we are too pleased with ourselves,
When our dreams have come true
Because we dreamed too little,
When we arrived safely
Because we sailed too close to
the shore.

Disturb us, Lord, when with the
Abundance of things we possess,
We have lost our thirst
For the waters of life;
Haven fallen in love with life,
We have ceased to dream of eternity
And in our efforts to build a new
Earth, we have allowed our vision
Of the new heaven to dim.

Disturb us, Lord, to dare more boldly,
To venture on wilder seas
Where storms will show your mastery;
Where losing sight of land,
We shall find the stars.

We ask you to push back
The horizon of our hopes;
And to push back the future
In strength, courage, hope, and love.

We ask in the name of our Captain,
Who is Jesus Christ.

JUL 6 1942

Two ships of our flotilla bombed, two killed, some hurt—ships did not sink.

JUL 7 1942

Raid cancelled. Gallant blokes were disappointed.

JUL 8 1942

General Roberts told men of 2nd Division they were best trained division in the Canadian Army and would get first chance to do a job if presented.

JUL 14 1942

Seven Day leave—Bastille Day in London- saw thousands of Free French on Parade, I followed them to Savoy Hotel on Strand.

De Gaulle the leader of Free French addresses liberty seeking Multitude.

I shook hands with him saying:
"Que Dieu vous benisse".
(God bless you.)
"Comment ca va?" il m'a dit.
How are you? he said to me
in English.

Evening—boarded train for Inverness Scotland—no berths, no snoring. Highland scenery majestic. Passed many a lonely shepherd's home.

JUL 18-19 1942

To Windermere, home and inspiration of William Wordsworth—Poet and Moralist. Visited his home—"Dove Cottage", the old church and tombstone. Saw house of Coleridge, also trudged 1500 feet up mountain to see remains of old sheep fold referred to in Wordsworth's pastoral poem Michael. Scenery beautiful, all gorgeous- Saw Blackpool in distance.

"Who comes not hither
Ne'er shall know
How beautiful   *Wordsworth*
The world below;"   *The Pass of Kirkstone*

JUL 21 1942

Saw Macbeth—well acted at Piccadilly Theatre. Evening back to forest.

AUG 2 1942

Second anniversary of our landing in Gourock on the Clyde River near Glasgow.

AUG 5 1942

Attended funeral in Brockwood Cemetery of Capt. Anderson, Walter's banker in Chatham.
600 white crosses here for Canadians. Over 500 of these were killed by motorcycles or trucks.

AUG 14 1942

Littlehampton—Town bombed killing Vicar, wife and six others. Bombing in Bognor Regis
two miles from us. We are bombed on all sides but escape. *"We must be born to be hanged."*
Shakespeare—The Tempest

AUG 18 1942

Swim in salt sea—three sirens today—no raids. 4th and 6th Bde. on scheme which developed
into Raid on Dieppe. If I knew it was real I would have been along. Chaplain's meeting
kept me home. Father Cote, Senior R.C. Chaplain, called meeting not knowing of Raid.
6 p.m.—T.L.C.'s seen from our window going east from Newhaven. We had a hunch it was
for France. I had practiced for Dieppe on intended raid and knew the town from maps and
air photos. Lieutenant Jim Palms had told me it was a land manouevre. He was killed.

AUG 19 1942

8 o'clock: Radio confirms our suspicions.
Noon :   Down to beach to find wounded and returning- no luck at
                   Chichester canal or beach.
5 o'clock: Saw bomber attacked by three spitfires—he jettisoned two bombs.

AUG 20 1942

Small groups come home with the tragic story of fierce opposition but gallant action. Major Turnbul makes me Colonel for afternoon. His brother Russ is missing. From the Essex Scottish, only 44 are accounted for, including just one attached officer- McRae. Morning requiem Mass for fallen and wounded. R.I.P.

AUG 21 1942

7:30 hrs: Another Mass at Littlehampton Convent for dead. Visited R.R.C. and R.H.L.I. to get locations of wounded.

Noon: Row upon row, ward after ward of battle casualties. Only a few Essex men and Captain McRae among wounded and many others of Brigade at No.1 Hospital Horsham.

18:00 hrs: To No.14 G.H. Horley- many wounded. Brought cigarettes, beads (rosaries) etc. to wounded.

Eve: Notified Regiments R.C.A. and 8th Recce. times of Sunday Masses.

9:30 hrs: Home for supper, Col. Mothersill new O.C.

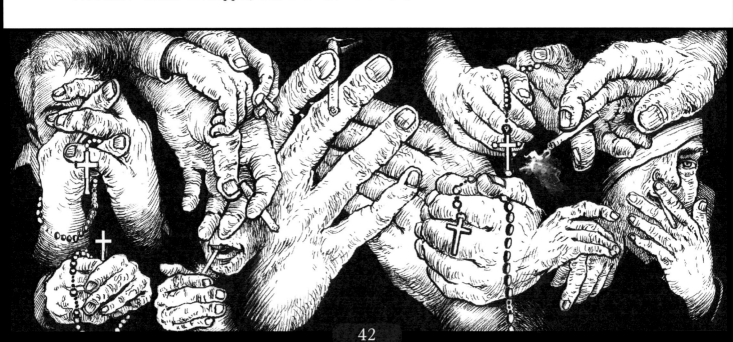

AUG 27 1942

All morning in Bramshot No.15 Hospital to see all the wounded. Identified Ray Belcourt in morgue accompanied by Jim, his brother.

Afternoon to #8 Canadian Hospital Aldershot. All have stories of heroism unparalleled in history of human relations, officers leading. Their parents must have been genuine to produce such men.

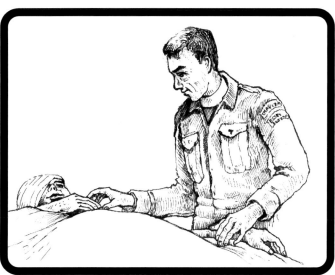

I'm glad to see you Padre, I'll take a blessing if you've got one for me, but I feel like I don't deserve it. I can't stop wondering why I was one of the lucky ones who made it back from Dieppe. This cut on my head is nothing. Most of our guys were shot to pieces. When I made it to the beach I was stepping in other guy's guts and blood—there was so much blood...

I wonder what the hell did I do to deserve making it back? So many of the other guys had families... I don't know if I'll ever get what I saw out of my mind. I see it every night—and I can still smell it—all over again—the faces—Padre I keep seeing those faces all covered in blood. Some of these guys in here are in a bad way Padre, and I don't mean just their injuries. You should hear it in here in the middle of the night. How are we ever going to live with this Padre?

AUG 19 1942 DIEPPE
Operation Jubilee

Editor's note

Of the 6,100 men in the Dieppe raid, 4,963 were Canadians. The Essex Scottish embarked 32 officers and 521 other ranks. Only two officers (who did not land) and 49 other ranks returned to England after the raid and of these 27 were wounded. Over 100 were killed or missing. 380 men were taken captive, many of them wounded, and eight men died while prisoners of war.

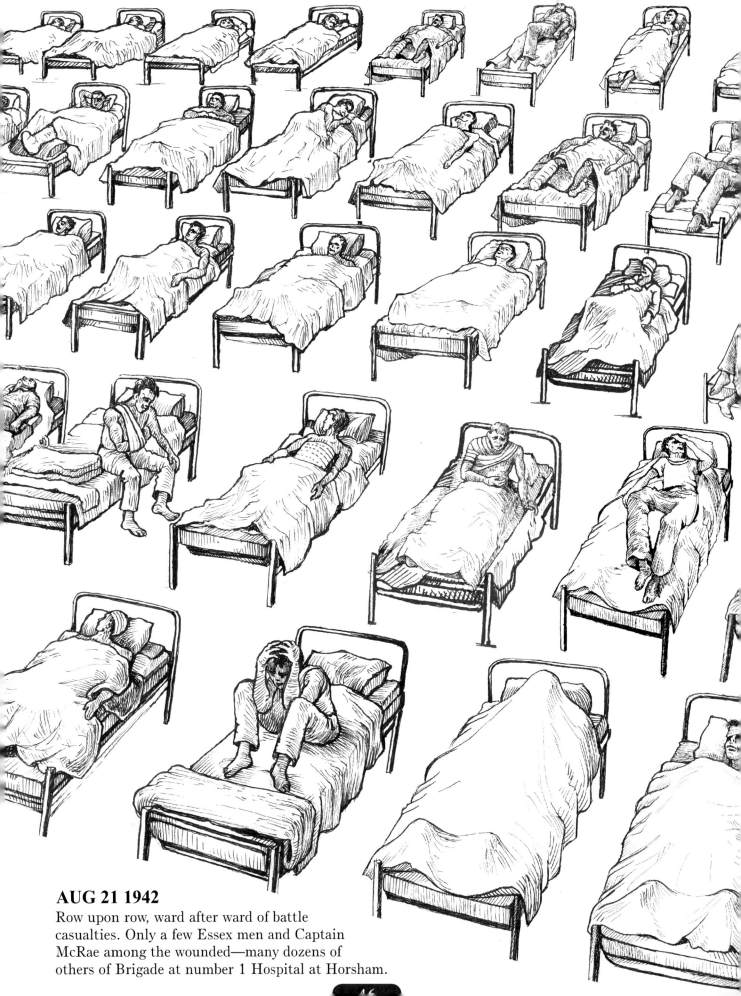

AUG 21 1942
Row upon row, ward after ward of battle
casualties. Only a few Essex men and Captain
McRae among the wounded—many dozens of
others of Brigade at number 1 Hospital at Horsham.

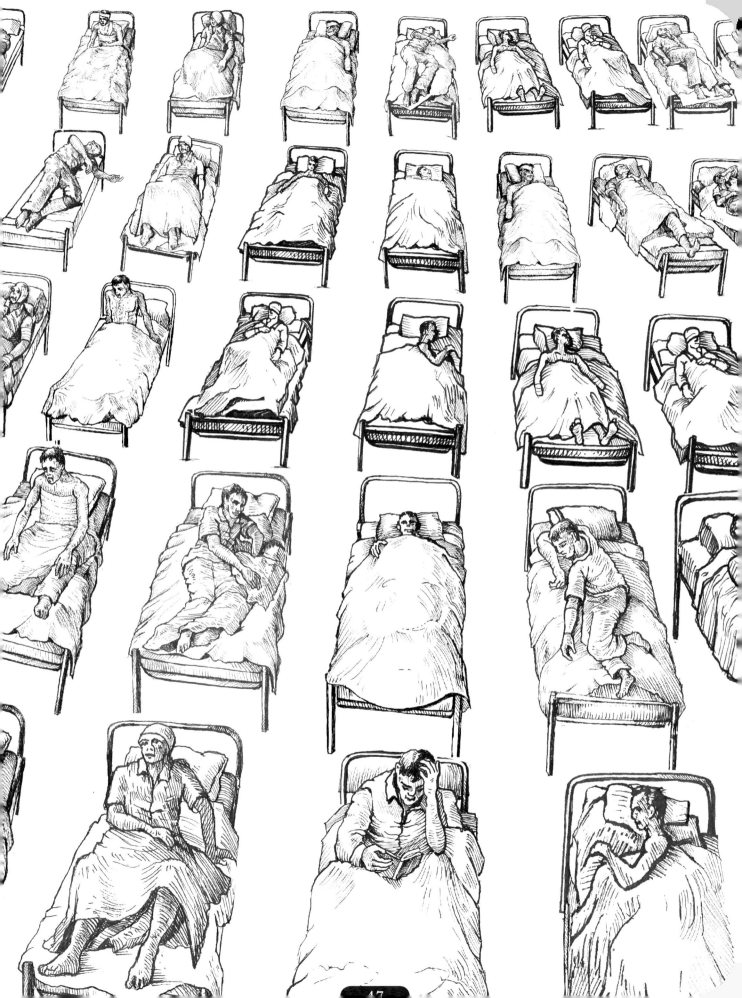

AUG 21 1942 The Tragedy of Dieppe

No Essex officers returned. Capt. McRae was attached from Glengarry Regt. Out of 30 officers who lived together at Aldershot and previously, I am the only original. Others had been transferred or shot down in France. Remnant of once proud gallant outfit are solemn but morale is high. Lads say they are glad I didn't go. I couldn't have done much good. In plan of United Nations, Dieppe maybe no tragedy, but blessing. I was Colonel for a day but forgot to collect a Colonel's pay.

AUG 1942 PADRE DALTON'S MEDITATION AFTER DIEPPE

SCENE I

On this balmy Sunday evening, the Padre glances with sombre thought yet legitimate price, across the turbulent English Channel- towards Dieppe where thousands of his fellow comrades purpled the sands with their noble blood. The genuine labors of Colonels Pearson, Jasperson and their assistants have borne fruit.

He had prayed with them, played with them, and trained with them, but being a non-combatant officer—was not allowed to fight with them.

Now those dear friends are somewhere on a foreign strand. We cannot visit them in hospitals or prisons or lay wreaths on their graves. That very thought prompts us to: "Remember all of them where remembrance is best".

SCENE II

Simultaneously our hearts go out to their next of kin. What do they think of war? What do we think of war? One memorable day robbed us of thousands of the flower of Canada's gallant manhood.

SCENE III

Being all volunteers, they bargained for the hazards of war and counted the cost. Their sacrifices were made, their battles fought in the heart and in the mind years before they became an accomplished fact in the theatre of operations. What do they think of war? Oh! That is the question. They realized that physical calamities are not wholly evil. It's the spiritual character that changes all. It's the intention that changes all. Thus purified, war is love undying—brilliant devotion to duty—participation in His war against evil things at Calvary.

St. Peter and Paul were cast into prison, but those who chained them lost the day. Those who chained other Peters and Pauls and Freds and Teds at Dieppe shall never win the day if all of us rededicate our lives as soldiers of Christ the King. In this sense, war against evil is splendid in the grandeur of that last sacrifice.

SCENE VI

Twilight is falling. The sound of marching feet interrupts meditation. They are not interested in defeat. The Padre studies them, their stalwart bearing and manly pride of stride. Among them are several who returned from the blood-bath of Dieppe. Some are carrying in their tunics invitations to Buckingham Palace, where the King will grant well merited awards for gallantry. Others are reinforcements who eagerly volunteered to close the ranks. They are trained and guided by that dauntless veteran of other battles that were fought and won- our new O.C. Lt.Col. J. Mothersill.

The roar of the waves seems to keep step as they echo back the undying challenge from Europe in Chains. "Close in the ranks". I heard Churchill in the House of Commons pronounce this. To safeguard the altars and hearts of those we left behind there must always be an Essex Scottish Regiment, God willing.

SUNDAY AUG 23 1942

I preached my shortest sermon. It was hard to face lads, so many empty seats, so many old reliables missing, but I asked for co-operation from remnant to build up new spirit, to close ranks and carry on. When we enlisted we bargained for hardships of war, but didn't realize we would miss our pals so much after almost three years of friendship. Through "Communion of Saints" they are still with us in spirit. Although only 44 of 550 Essex Scottish who invaded, returned, personal loss is nation's gain, (we hope).

All officers march past in single file to salute the huge grave of gallant men. It was the largest military funeral in history of Brookwood Cemetery. Forty Canadians from Dieppe, buried side by side, with 600 casualties of former accidents. Twelve Generals, many Brigadiers, hundreds of officers, men and Chaplains were present. Generals McNaughton, Crerar, Roberts etc. were present.

SUNDAY AUG 23 1942

Evening to 2 C.C. to see more wounded in Hospital.

AUG 24 1942

Visited remnant of Dieppe men and wrote letters to next of kin. Of course my next of kin letters included non-Catholics. Getting acquainted with new men from reinforcement units. Cabled sister Margaret some days before- safe in England.

AUG 24 1942

Evening: Visited men in klink saying: "Men this reminds me of Dieppe." They got it. (They should have been on the job). Fr. Cote brings 2,500 Canadian cigarettes.

Bless me father for I have sinned....for these and all my past sins I am truly sorry, mostly Padre I'm just so damned ashamed of myself for being locked up in here when the Regiment got so shot up in Dieppe. I sure as hell never planned this. How the hell can I tell anybody back home where I was on Aug 19 ? I told you before about my drinking and fighting- yeah- I was locked up before. I never used to be like this Padre, but I got a letter telling me my wife was stepping out with the neighbor. I thought everything was OK when I left home but now she is all I can think about- she hasn't answered any of my letters. Padre it's a shitty excuse but when I drink I just get so damned angry I end up picking a fight just so I can hit somebody. Yeah, as you can see I usually get the worst of it. Padre, if you can, help me get out of here- I've gotta make up for this. Most of all I don't know how I can look at any of those guys in the eye... I mean the ones who made it back.

AUG 26 1942

Wrote parents of Ray Belcourt and Lieutenant Palms. Cable from brother Walt that I was reported missing. Louis, my Batman, replied "All's well". He stretched the truth.

AUG 27 1942

Visited H.Q. Anti-tank with church parade orders. Noon: contacted new men of two Co.'s. Still writing 600 letters to next of kin. Letters commence coming from next of kin.

> Dear Rev. Captain Dalton:
>   Received your very lovely and thoughtful letter. Many thanks for your kind words. How it does help.
>   You have given me so much faith, courage and hope, just like you have given our boys, something they'll never forget or lose.
>   Ed was always cheerful, yes a real soldier, thanks to you Father, for you have done a fine job for our boys. So I'm not worrying, for I must be brave as he was.
>
>   Yours truly,
>   Mrs. Eugene Surgeon

AUG 28 1942

Morning: R.Reg.C., then the Essex klink. Later visiting new men and officers. A memory test remembering names and home towns, must start all over again. 10:30: British bomber crashed ½ mile away. Pilot killed.

Editor's note
The term "klink" was Mike's favorite term for a jail or detention center.

AUG 29 1942
Morning:　　H.Q. Two men want marriage advice.
11:00 hrs:　Called to office of Colonel Mothersill. He asked me to get information
　　　　　　from wounded in hospitals concerning acts of gallantry of their comrades.

Padre you asked about acts of gallantry. Well you would have been proud as hell if you could have seen our guys. It seemed impossible to get from the water to the shore and then find some protection, but the guys just charged ahead. If you asked me they all performed those acts of gallantry. I took this damned bullet in the hip even before I had a chance to get off the ramp. I couldn't walk. Now I wonder if I would have had the guts to do what the other guys did. We were stuck in the rocks and sand for a while and I was surrounded by guys who were dead or dying and I could see the guys on shore... They never had a chance and all I could do was watch. Now when I talk about it or even think about it I feel like puking. I could give you the names of my whole platoon, but they were all dead before they could get onto the beach. What the hell am I gonna do now?

Padre, you have heard about that other Padre Rev. Foote—what a guy—I was just lying there, I couldn't move. He came along all covered in blood, I told him I'm OK—said help somebody who was losing blood. He said: "I'll be back" and then he just went back and forth from the water to the landing craft over and over again. I saw him go up and down the beach. He saved so many. I passed out but I think it was Foote who must have carried me to the water. Then I heard that he chose to stay with the guys—if that's not gallantry I don't know what is. Now they're all in some stinkin POW camp. Damn Padre how could the big shots not know what things were like over there? The Germans must have thought we were crazy. We never had a chance. Why didn't we get some more artillery and air support? What a stinkin waste of lives. What was the raid for anyway?

AUG 30 1942
To Cinema—Dieppe News Reel. Recognized Capt.Kennedy and some lads of R.Reg.C.

AUG 31 1942
To No.7 Can. G.H. Birmingham to visit Brig. Lett wounded at Dieppe; Lorimer lost
a leg, Culpan shot through lung. Row upon row of battle casualties. All in good spirits.
Saw Macbeth at Piccadilly Theatre. London still busy. Coventry bomb damage great.

SEP 2 1942
9 o'clock: To R.Reg., 11th Fd. Ambulance at three locations. Dinner at Bde.H.Q. Then
to Anti-Tank and B.O.R. and Essex klink. Met new Colonels Hurley and Fraser. Calls to
arrange national Day of Prayer. Evening Confessions in Y.M.C.A. Air mail letters in from
Canada- answered immediately. Even army beds are welcome at late ends of these busy days.

Dear Father:
I wish to thank you for your comforting and inspiring letter. It was most certainly a message of hope and consolation, and coming as it did from one who was so close to our boys in that terrible hour, it was a great consolation.
I have now official word that my son Fred is a prisoner of war.
Very truly yours,
Mrs. B. Lyons.

Dear Father Dalton:
Jack and George over there with you are good boys, and Bert, well I was grieved and also proud and honored. I had a son that the Lord thought was worthy enough to die for his king and country.
When the Almighty loaned me my sons I knew when he wanted them, he would call them home. I do not feel that my son is gone from me. I feel that he is right here with me, as I write this letter, and he has just gone to prepare a place for all of us. I was fortunate that God loaned him to me for 21 years.
Father please talk to Jack and George, and try to make them not think of revenge. God knows best.
Thanks again for your kindness and prayers.
Helena M. Leopold

SEP 2 1942
Just found letter from mother of a soldier killed in action. She wrote:
"If I ever get my hands on that so-and-so Hitler..." The boys would
gladly arrange a meeting and referee the match, and put bets on it too.

SEP 3 1942

National Day of Prayer—6:30 Mass for Essex Scottish, 8:00 hear Confessions. 80 attended. I bought their breakfast in café. 10:00 parish Mass at Arundel. I helped pastor hear Confessions. Protestant officer brought Laundry No. 3 Unit to church.

SEP 4 1942

20:00 hrs. Conferred with Protestant Padre regarding letters to next of kin. Lord Haw-Haw from German radio; "Send over 50 Essex Scottish and we'll have the Regiment up to strength". It was a clue they had many prisoners—first evidence.

SEP 8 1942

Wrote letters to next of kin. Saw picture of our men in prison. It was dropped by Germany as propaganda. Recognized Flatt brothers, Alex Montro, Hilborn, Johnson, Echer, Bud Heaton, Thibert, Cecil Gulliver, Abbott, Cyril DeWulf, Mike Boyer, Cecil Carol, Dan Conley, M. J. Lemmon.
Notified brother Walter air-mail to tell Flatt parents in Detroit that their boys are alive.

SEP 12 1942

Tony Horlick R.H.L.I. plunges into fast Aron river to bring girl 100 yards back, saving her life. He received a parliament mention and parchment in England.
He was also mentioned in Brigade Orders.

SEP 18 1942

Frs Cote, Gehl and myself hear Confessions at 33 Laundry Littlehampton. One month ago today Canadians set off for Dieppe. One month of fond memories went by quickly because I was busy. I wonder where the old gang are tonight; the old gang of three years total friendship. "Dona eis requiem sempiteram." *(Give them eternal rest.)*

SEP 22–26 1942

Attended lectures at Oxford University on International Relations and lived and dined with students and professors at Jesus College which Lawrence of Arabia attended. Heard Mendelson's 49th Song Without Words at Lady Margaret Hall. Saw Merchant of Venice and Madame Butterfly in London performances.

Bought portable gramophone for seven pds.
First records bought were:
Panis Angelicus by John McCormack
Bless this House by John McCormack
Londonderry Air by Kreisler
Ave Maria and Agnus Dei
Pride of County Down
I Hear you Calling
and Largo by Handel.

OCT 9 1942
Canadians put in chains at Dieppe. *Editor's note: Canadians were in Stalag VIII in Germany.*

OCT 11 1942
Where were our lads last night? Canada puts German prisoners in chains.

OCT 18 1942
Protestant Chaplin Jack Chandler comes to get a copy of Next of Kin letter. He wants to discuss with his platoon "the Soldier is a Monk". Such tremendous trifles, if considered in every platoon of the Canadian Army, would transform Army into chivalrous Knights.

OCT 21 1942
All afternoon recording names of prisoners of Dieppe. Electric fireplace out.
Too cold to write more. And so to bed, 10:30, to rest, to sleep, helmet at side, and perchance to dream, till Louis comes in to put up the blackout at 6:30 a.m. And so commences another busy day in search of souls—in search of Victory.

OCT 27 1942
I hopped into a taxi at Victoria station, London saying "Take me to see King George". Driver needed convincing but landed me at Buckingham Palace. I was 15 feet in front of King George VI as he decorated heros of Dieppe. It's a nice palace. He's a nice King. Liz wasn't there. We dined at Lyons restaurant on Piccadilly. Three sirens today—no hits.

OCT 28 1942
Saw King Henry IV—Atkins played Falstaff. Englishmen are born actors. They are acting all the time. Furniture and setting of Shakespeare's time make stage realistic. Back to Middleton with more lads waiting for me to help them get married or get out of it. Some can't get along with women or can't get along without them. The only advice to give in this case: "whether you marry or not, you'll regret it." They do.

NOV 3 1942
Route march after dinner—11 miles with support company. March through autumn woods was invigorating. We marched in shadow of famous Duke of Norfolk's Church at Arundel. We bought a few oranges on the way. Sergeant Hussey M.M. at Dieppe said it was the first orange he had in England. Several new men fall out with blistered feet.

Says I: *"One impulse from a vernal wood*
            Can teach you more of man,
            Of moral evil and good,
            Than all the sages can." – Wordsworth

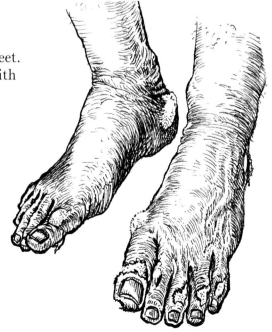

Says they: You can't teach poetry Padre to blistered feet.
Says I: Wordsworth didn't have to march route with
            pack. But Joyce Kilmer did and wrote:

            "My shoulders ache beneath my pack
            Lie easier cross upon his back."

Sgt. Joyce Kilmer was a convert in 'Fighting 69th' of New York—killed in action in France in 1918. Added I: As he trudged along the muddy fields of France of Victory, death and glory immortal— so let us all trudge along the highways and byways of this brave little island fortress till the day when we shall loosen the fetters of Europe in chains. I carried equipment of young Joe Schumaker of Kitchener, who developed sore feet. He's young, so he'll be up and at it tomorrow at Reveille.

NOV 5 1942

Two sirens in morning. 9000 German prisoners in desert. Germans on the run- rates with best news of the war. Cold, damp, wet, rainy day but spirits are as high as bombers overhead.

NOV 11 1942

R.Reg C. all day. Tea with Father Pitts in Littlehampton. He composes his own music for masses and is the organist. He produced many rough copies in pencil showing corrections when muses deceived him. He played original and corrections on piano. I got a fleeting glimpse of struggling genius of a Mozart, Mendelssohn, Chopin etc. No one fell out in a 20 mile route march. The Battle of Egypt is an inspiration for our tired feet and minds.

NOV 18 1942

Arundel Park—An Irish American wrapped himself around a few Scotch Whiskies and then attempted to wrap his 'Jeep" going 50, around an airplane trailer. He did. Unwrapping both, they found the Jeep beyond repair and Irish with a whole bunch of broken legs. MORAL—stay on the "Haw" side of the road in England. By coincidence, I received a box of Scapular Medals from his mother the same day. I shall now proceed to Horsham Hospital to wrap them around what is left of his neck. *Editor's note*

"Haw" is the command to a horse to turn to the left. To turn to the right the command is: "Gee".

NOV 21 1952

Met Anglican Vicar. Evening to a converted Chapel and a Catholic Library at Y.M.C.A. where I hear Confessions.

...but Father I can't wait ...

.... I know you have to get some sleep but I'll be quick....I just need to tell somebody. I need your help Padre. I was in Dieppe and you know how everybody is so God damned mad about it all and how we all feel so bad about all our old gang getting killed or captured...I don't know how to say it but I need your help to stop hating these new guys. I'm not like you Padre. I can't forget. I don't mean that you forget our guys, but you seem to be able to get over it. I don't think I ever will but I really hate these new guys—when they laugh I feel as if they don't have the right to do so... and I have come so close to smashing some of their heads in... it's stupid I know, but it's as if they don't give a shit about what happened to my platoon, or our whole damned regiment...Christ Padre I know I must sound like a crazy man but I have to stop hating these bastards or I'll kill some of them. It's been two months and I can't even stand to look at them. I know you have talked about closing ranks and accepting the new guys and doing it for the sake of those who died and honoring their memory and all that... Ah hell —Padre I wish I'd died over there—I came over on the same boat as you and now you are the only guy I really know... I think I know what you are going to say... but I will listen—sorry to put you through this. I don't know how you can stand to listen to all these guys, so many of us are damned near crazy. Padre, I don't know if I can get through all this....

NOV 21 1942

Anglican Vicar will give us his church organ to be carried to his church hall
for Mass each Sunday—Ecumenism.

NOV 23 1942

Field court martial. Called for character witness. Waited all day—slow judge.

I'm glad to see you here Padre. Sometimes I feel I have to talk to someone other than the other officers—and someone who knows how to keep his mouth shut. This court martial business is a bloody waste of time, but since we have to be here and I know you remember all the men, maybe you can help me with something. It's got nothing to do with this case.

You know one of my men got killed in training a few days ago. It was another accident and we've had lots of those, but this one didn't need to have happened. If the soldier hadn't been so hesitant and had trusted and listened to the guys with him, he'd be alive today—he didn't grab for the rope until it was out of his reach—just damned lucky he didn't fall on one of the other guys.

What's bothering me is wondering if it was my fault—but dammit, I couldn't exempt him from the training exercise—could I? He was one of those guys who was never on a team of any sort, and you know how you have to learn to work with your team here. It's life or death. We've all heard you call them warriors, but some of them act like damned sissies and I don't know what to do with them. Most of them will be great soldiers—brave as hell, makes me sick to think that some of them are never going to grow up...

I don't know Padre, they are all just kids—some still need their mothers to be looking after them. They think I'm a mean son of a bitch but you know I'm just trying to keep them alive. Damn it to hell Padre, some of them will be useless in action and if they survive, this is going to ruin some of them for life- just like a lot of those old guys who came home from WWI as wrecks. I don't know why the hell these young men volunteered for this anyway. The other officers tell me to forget it, but I can't. I can't stop thinking that maybe I'm not cut out for this job. I wonder how the boys will be in combat—yeah, but I also wonder how I'll be too. Looks like my turn to testify. Maybe we can talk later. Thanks for listening Padre.

NOV 25 1942

No.7 Canadian Hospital—Birmingham. Met Anglican Vicar. Evening to a
converted Chapel and Catholic Library at Y.M.C.A. where I hear Confessions.

NOV 25 1942

Thousands flock into Westminster Abbey for the first time in 900 years of its history. I pause awhile, then onto Westminster Cathedral.

NOV 25 1942

2 o'clock: Back to Abbey to hear American choir broadcast to the United States.

5 o'clock: Saw bacon and eggs on the screen for the price of a cinema. I'm going back.

6 o'clock: Royal Opera House in Covent Garden. There is no opera here in war time. It is a dance hall for troops at six pence.

Westminster Abbey

Westminster Cathedral

NOV 26 1942

Number 7 Canadian Hospital Birmingham. Mickey Lorimer forgot one leg at Dieppe but he and Lecouter (wounded) are in good spirits. Saw London filled with Americans for their Thanksgiving Ceremonies. Thousands in every street salute the King's Commission, and I was thrilled to return the salute to the vigorous American Army. Roosevelt's Proclamation rings through the hallowed halls of Westminster.

Excerpt from Roosevelt's Proclamation 2571

The final months of this year, now almost spent, find our Republic and the nations joined with it waging a battle on many fronts for the preservation of liberty.
Now therefore, I, Franklin D. Roosevelt, President of The United States of America, do hereby invite the attention of the people to the joint resolution of Congress approved December 26, 1941, which designates the fourth Thursday in November of each year as Thanksgiving Day; and I request that both Thanksgiving Day, November 26, 1942, and New Years Day, January 1, 1943, be observed in prayer publicly and privately.

NOV 27 1942

R.H.L.I. Doug McCann killed—Intended to be married soon.

NOV 28 1942

Streets of London busy. All bustling to and from their war jobs, except the singing gals strolling along Piccadilly—
* "wid er' fixed glad eye and er' vacant stare". Signs on bombed buildings seem equally appropriate for them- "Open for Business".

* *Editor's note*
From poem "Gal of the Streets" by Padre Rev. Geoffrey Studdert Kennedy, nicknamed 'Woodbine Wille' by soldiers in WWI. Poem from his collection: 'The Unutterable Beauty'.

DEC 13 1942

Leave on Isle of Man. Scenery and climate similar to Eire. Italian interns seemed contented behind bars. I attended a session of court of Justice at Peace. Governor of Isle married the sister of Queen Elizabeth. I saw her at the Club where I stayed.

DEC 24 1942

Officers' party Christmas Eve., Midnight Mass. Col J. Mothersill, Major B. MacDonald 2nd in command, Capt. Lund, Adjutant, Major Jones, Brigade Staff Capt., Capts. Wansbrough, Kealy and other non-Catholics attended and helped singing. I had two Masses the next day for other units. Confessions in all units from noon till midnight.

Bless me father for I have sinned. Padre I'm not Catholic, I just hear the guys saying that. It seems to take a load off their mind. Now, maybe because it's Christmas, I have to get something off my mind. Padre I'm sorry I treated some of our guys so badly. I guess that's a guilty conscience. Now most of those guys are dead or in some stinking POW camp and I'm being sent home. They say I'm not fit for action. I'm relieved that I'm leaving but I feel like I should stay. The hell of it is I don't even remember the dreams. I just wake up screaming. It's what I can't stop thinking about when I'm awake. You can see I shake all the time and I just can't seem to stop- can't eat- can't sleep- feel like puking all the time...

It started after Dieppe. The medic said it would go away, but it's like a movie playing in my head all the time. When we got to the beach I remember getting ready to go down the ramp and suddenly blood and something mushy and hot hit me in the face. The guy who was ahead of me was Bill. You know him. He came flying back on top of me. He must have taken a bullet just under the brim of his helmet. His blood and brains were all over me and then another guy came down on top of both of us. I think it was Phil, you know him too. I could see blood gushing out of his neck but I couldn't move out of the way, they were just too damned heavy.

I was soaked in their blood Padre not mine. I could taste it and smell it. I was choking and gagging on my own vomit too, then another guy fell on all of us- it was hell. I just couldn't get up and there was nobody to help. Then the ramp went up and we headed back for the ship I guess. I was screaming to let me off, but my helmet was full of blood and my face was all covered in it and they must have thought I was shot and going crazy. I still don't feel like I got all the blood out of my hair. Maybe I am crazy now but I wasn't then; if only they had let me get to the beach like the other guys I'd be alright now. Yeah or maybe I'd be dead or in a POW camp, but anything would be better than this. Now I feel like some God damned useless coward- that's what other people will think too. How the hell can I tell anybody back home what happened?... Why I'm like this? I don't even have any wounds... for months I wished I could go home... and now...

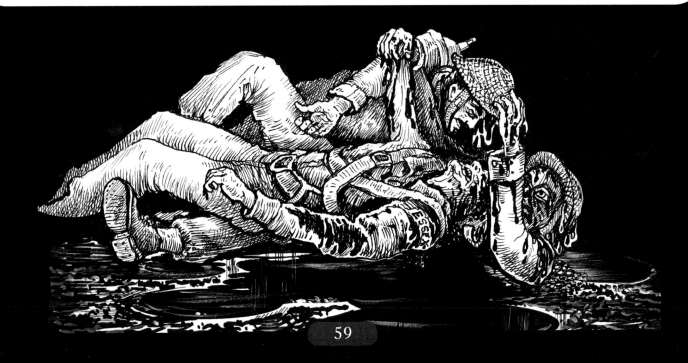

DEC 24 1942

Saw most of men at their turkey banquet. All O.K. No bombs heard. Mail and parcels galore.
I got 20 Christmas boxes and 20,000 cigarettes. I looked up lads who didn't get any boxes.

"Their faces were wreathed with smiles and their
hearts with mirth made lighter"   George Vandenhoff 1820–1885

DEC 30 1942

I have seen England from the air. I have seen Scotland, Ireland and Eire, by train, bus
and thousands of miles on foot, which is best. From Ford Air Port near Bognor Regis, we
took off in a new Beaufighter- twin engine aircraft. Our winter quarters at Middleton took
on an air of romance, winding roads, well kept gardens etc. English Chanel was rough.
Trip was uneventful, apart from the fact that a motor developed trouble. We hit the dirt
going 120 miles an hour (about average landing speed). Pilot
was Wing Commander Braham age 22, son of an Anglican
Vicar. He won the D.S.O. in a scrap over the North Sea
and saw the majority of the R.A.F. go down nobly in
the Battle of Britain. He invited me back next week for
a longer trip. Flying is relaxing. No wonder the birds
sing better than man. I wore a harness and a parachute.

DEC 30 1942

Midnight: Mass at Littlehampton for number 3 Mobile Laundry.
0845   : Mass January 1st 1943 for Essex Scottish.
10:00   : Mass for R.H.L.I. January 1st 1943.
Midnight Mass at New Years is custom in Montreal where most men come from.

JAN 3 1943

3 o'clock: 20,000 cigarettes arrived from St Alphonsus Holy Name, which was 500 strong
when I left. They won't last long among over 3000 in 4th Brigade and area. Sirens sound
and warn us of enemy action. From my top floor billet I look over roofs of small town of
Middleton to Ford Airport about ¼ mile away. In succession the fighters take off and
circle the area. All clear shortly. If it wasn't for unfinished business at my desk, I would
have been in the air to meet Germans. Corporal Mason had arranged a ride at two o'clock.

JAN 9 1943

Two records just arrived from Detroit: "Rose of Tralee" and "Danny Boy" sung by my brother
Walter, speech by my sister Antoinette and the children: "Holy Night", introduction by Anne
Marie. All come in clear, a thrill to hear their voices after *"Wandering on a foreign strand"*.
Sir Walter Scott

JAN 12 1943

Let's go up above the clouds to get to the setting of the R.A.F. "Never was so much owed to so few by so many". (words by Churchill). Wing Commander Braham, aged 22 one of the youngest, is equivalent to Lieutenant Colonel. This time he gave me ear phones as he described our height, position, etc. From 9000 feet he dove going 320 m.p.h. (400 is the maximum for this Beaufighter) to test his cannons and machines guns. These long range fighters are among the fastest in the world. Axis planes included 20 tons of steel and metal going 400 miles an hour and can spit 700 lbs of lead in 12 seconds says Corporal Don Mason. Nothing can live in its path. The Channel churned under the impact. The sun shone clear. At 20 miles from shore opposite Le Havre we were enveloped totally by

fog and rain. The most part of an hour was blind flying. Alone in the clouds, I thought of the courage of the R.A.F. when rain becomes ice over enemy territory. I thought of genius of man to have invented all the gadgets. Directions from the ground crew were ill advised and even though Braham was the son of a Cambridge Parson he told him so. Coming out of a cloud we saw the ground coming up to meet us twenty feet distant, so he says, on the side of a hill. He "gave her the works". Up went the elevator into obscurity. He told the dumb bloke on the ground he would find his own way in.

There is a fascination, I believe, controlling 20 tons in the air. If any man likes flying he is relaxed. I'm up again "lost in the clouds" twixt heaven and earth, with not a care in the world, not even a thought of getting my money back if my parachute didn't open. It's good for mind, soul, and body to have a total change after 3½ years of total war. I shall always remember the privilege of riding with the young veteran.

JAN 19 1943

Many leave for Scotland T.L.C. training. 4 o'clock Tea at home of Sir Richard and Lady Gregory. He is a scientist and writer. In his huge library he was busy composing a book on natural ethics.

JAN 20 1943

Packing up for 19th move in England. Therefore I know 18 areas as well as I do Kingsbridge. Louis packs jeep up to the roof. We made it without using four wheel drive. Dinner at Brigade.

JAN 21 1943

Now live at Brigade H.Q. in Slindon to be central to 700 R.C. men of war in my area. They put me in the 'Bull-pen' with four combat Officers. I was just unpacking when Major Don Mingay says: "the Padre gets a room for himself." Everybody rushes. Officers are moved and my small room is ready.
There's an example of Protestant action for a Catholic priest. 150 men now live in the house of one big shot and his maids, gardeners, cockneys etc.

JAN 31 1943

Louis on 48 hr leave. Rain. Rain. Rain. I paddle jeep home from Middleton and put it under a tree, jump out in the blackness into a sea of mud- low shoes- new suit. Many wheat fields flooded, roads overrun. One redeeming feature is- rain isn't fog.

FEB 5 1943

2:10 o'clock—all doors in massive Slindon Manor rattle three times in quick succession. Many rush to roof to see smoke of bombs at Bognor six miles away. I met caretaker today. Says he:"Visit Anglican Church here and find plaque telling of death of Stephen Langton". Steve was the Archbishop of Canterbury who put pressure on King John II to sign the 'Magna Carta' at Runnymede. Reverend Stephen got results for common man which we still enjoy in English speaking world. We are in a Total War to defend those rights. History of this joint goes back 1000 years. It was formerly a monastery.

FEB 6 1943

To Bognor Regis to get suit at cleaners. Plate glass on downtown stores gone for blocks in bombing raid. Louis could walk in through the window instead of the door. Suit was undamaged. Dr. Cloutier M.O., Corporals Jim Donal, Steve Chamko and other Essex lads help in rescue work after bombing. They bring some out alive, some dead.

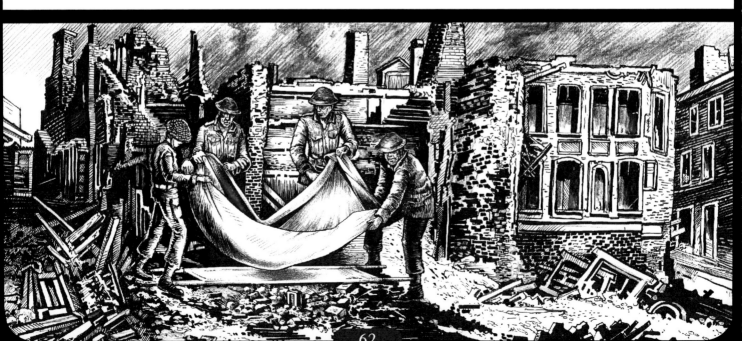

FEB 17 1943

To 2nd Division Snipers School. Germans at Dieppe were good snipers. They picked off many officers.

FEB 26 1943

Scheme: "Elm". Slept out in a 19 acre field in February with frost on ground. It is usually raining. To bed at 2 a.m., then up at 5:30 a.m. I prayed for Reveille so I could get up and get warm.

MAR 1 1943

Two week's maneuvers for all Canadian Army. Fought our way up beyond Oxford to encounter British tanks. Weather dry but cold in jeep without curtains. Slept out usually beside car. Found shelter in old barns a few nights. Little sleep as moves were mostly at night. Bully beef and biscuits are not objectionable when there is nothing else for days. Men came back in good spirits and health.

MAR 23 1943

From March 14–22nd on leave in Dublin Eire. Said Mass in Protestant Cathedral.

APR 9 1943

Message from: Senior Chaplain H.Q. 2nd Division, to Major Dalton "Congratulations for promotion due to fine priestly service". For several days and nights we hear bombers going to Germany in the biggest raids of all times.

APR 9 1943

4th Brigade Officers are raising Cain with me for being improperly dressed. I still wear Captain's three 'pips' instead of Major's crown on shoulders. I can't buy any here. There is only one store in Slindon. Steve Martin in Kingsbridge has a larger stock. As soon as I get an "Anchor" I'll put the "Crowns" up.

Officer's Shoulder Epaulets

Captain

Second in command of a company or a sub-unit of up to 120 men

Major

Usually in command of a company or dealt with administrative affairs

APR 20 1943

7 o'clock Mass for nuns at Arundel Castle. Four Padre hours after for different companies. I talked on our Senior Padre, killed in action, mentioned in dispatches, and read a letter from one who was with him on the battlefield—St. John the Apostle. In those days the Padre was commander in Chief Jesus Christ.

EASTER SUNDAY

Communicants more numerous than any other Sunday in Army. Spiritual mobilization for Victory and Peace, with Justice and Charity gaining ground. Same old weapons used in day of St. Paul- helmet of Faith, breast plate of Justice, etc.

MAY 30 1943

Moved to Halnacker House—20th move in England. From my private room I see majestic stately steeple of Chichester Anglican Cathedral four miles away. I tell men historic significance of this new area as I do on every new move.

Spring 1943

On the first day I wore the Major's crown I said two Masses on a week
day. The second at 4:30 in afternoon at No.3 F.D.S., then at Bognor
in the evening. Four units were represented. I now also have 12 Padre
hours weekly in all units. Wow! I thought I was busy before. Boys like it.

```
Major Michael Joseph Dalton, B.A., M.B.E
          R. C. Chaplain to

4th Canadian Infantry Brigade - Comprising

        4th BRIGADE HEADQUARTERS

        ESSEX SCOTTISH INFANTRY

        ROYAL REGIMENT OF CANADA

        ROYAL HAMILTON LIGHT INFANTRY

     2nd FIELD COMPANY ENGINEERS R.C.E.

  "B" COMPANY TORONTO SCOTS (MACHINE GUNNERS)

     4th BRIGADE WORKSHOP R.C.O.C.

        No. 3 LAUNDRY & MOBILE BATH

           11th FIELD AMBULANCE

              No. 3 F. O. S.

           ATTACHED TROOPS

        AND TROOPS IN AREA
```

Editor's note
This list is copied directly
from the diary

JUN 14 1943

Letter from Central Chancery of the Order of Knighthood, St. James Palace:

> "The King has been graciously pleased on the advice of Canadian Ministers to give orders for the following appointment of the:
>
> ## 'Most Excellent Order of the British Empire'
>
> To be additional member of the Military Division of the said most excellent Order:
>
> **Major Michael Joseph Morgan Dalton M.B.E. Canadian Chaplain Service.**

Officers say M.B.E. Means 'Mike's Bloody Effort'. H.Q. wants to know if I'll be available on July 13 to receive a Medal from the King. I say: "OK". (I'll try anything once).

JUN 10 1943

Banquet at Unicorn Hotel Chichester. Farewell for good old C.O. Jack Mothersill. Col. Bruce McDonald takes command. Col. Pearson C.B.E. speaker among others. This was the first day I wore the M.B.E. ribbon. According to custom they drink to my health of body and soul (but not pocket book). I get honour of paying for drinks.

JUN 12 1943

Attended House of Commons. Anthony Eden spoke, also Atlee- deputy Prime Minister. Lloyd George last war Prime Minister is 85, but looks bright and alert. To House of Lords in afternoon; Lord Simon spoke. I noticed Duke of Norfolk present.

JUN 25 1943

Visited Clubland on East Side London in slums on the bus through bombed miles of east end. Youth there 14 to 18 have their own Parliament.

JUL 7 1943

Bde. officers beat sergeants in softball game. I got a home run and one other hit. Not bad for a Padre on the wrong side of 40.

JUL 8 1943

Two tickets arrive for guests to Buckingham Palace. One goes to my trusty batman, Louis, the other to George Gynn, Y.M.C.A. Supervisor.

JUL 10 1943

Radio announces First Canadian division invaded Italy. Boys are cheered- a second front. Let's get this bloody business over with and get home. News flash announces successful landing according to plan. (They smelt macaroni I suppose.)
We are living in the presence of history. Day of Liberation commences July 10th. It was first Division's turn to take a whirl at it. Good luck boys. As band played 'Oh Canada' I thought of lads in Italy. Never did that patriotic theme strike a more responsive chord as at a sports meeting. While they were scrapping on a foreign strand, Brigadier Segar took two Captains and myself to Canadian army sports finals at Aldershott. Mrs McNuaghton gave out prizes, 2nd Division way out in front- as usual. We are now champs of Canadian Army.
Our day of sports is just as essential as their day of fighting.

JUL 11 1943

Prayers at Mass for success of our fellow Canadians. General Communion for fallen R.I.P. That's a good chance to encourage the lads to go to Confession and Communion.
("Have pity on me at least you my friends.") Job 19:21

JUL 13 1943 The Padre invades bloodlessly Buckingham Palace London.

Famous paintings hang in massive halls. Three hundred Navy, Air, Army and Civilians to be decorated, chat of their various experiences on the Battle fronts of the World, Nurses and A.T.S. also. Those to be Knighted knelt before the King. He placed a sword on each shoulder saying, I suppose "Good Knight" at 11 o'clock in the morning. About 1000 witnessed the show. The King's "caller off" rings out each name and the decoration before he appears before him. All come up in single file, in the manner the men line up for dinner in the camp, with mess tins.

The thought occurred to me that I might have been lining up in Stalag Germany with most of the Essex Scottish for sauerkraut and lager. It also came to my fancy that this was a big stretch from the mud of Chichester Camps, but my batman had everything all cleaned up and worked on my Sam Brown for a week.

George VI: "How long have you been over?"
I answered: "3 years"
George VI: "I suppose the Canadians are glad they have a job to do at last?"
I answered: "That's right your Majesty."

Member of the Order of The British Empire Medal

If he asked me where I was from I was all set to say "Kingsbridge". He put the Medal M.B.E. on my chest, shook hands, and smiled. I stepped back, bowed and down the runway walked.
Kingsbridge north of Goderich is my old schoolhouse. Some of his Majesty's body guards all in red wore enough medals to choke a cow. (I guess that's why they are called "Beefeaters"). My batman Louis had a ringside seat for the show.

"Ladies and Gentlemen. The King." God save the King.

Padre Mike and some of his 'Lads'
at Buckingham Palace

JUL 13 1943

I called on the Senior R.C. Chaplain at his office on Trafalgar Square. All he would tell me about why I received the medal was—it was the custom to accept these medals as they come along. The Holy Ghost must have done some "groaning".

JUL 14 1943

Shipley near Horsham, coming home I called upon one of the world's greatest historians and Catholic laymen, whose books we studied in Seminary. Hillaire Belloc is a genius. He is a great creator of thought. He is now feeble at 72, but reminded me of Dad with his grey beard, as he came out to wave goodbye.

JUL 16 1943

To Cathedral where Churchill delivered eulogy for Polish General Sikorski. Churchill didn't know I was there. He knelt up front and followed Funeral Mass with book. I went back to the barracks and said to the lads: "I saw the old man on his knees".

JUL 22 1943

Padre hour at Singleton for the lads who fix our trucks, then 15 miles to Littlehampton for Padre Hour for No.2 Laundry, the lads who fix our blankets.

JUL 23 1943

To dentist... nuff said. Wheat and oats cut in vicinity.

JUL 27 1943

Days too busy to record at night the incongruities of time and place that make Drama. I went to Slindon to see if our garden was progressing. Things grow quicker due to moisture. Plums were ripe. So are our appetites since fruit not sufficient for normal ration.

JUL 29 1943

Mussolini resigns! One dictator down two to go. Canadian mail in, tobacco from my sister Tonette. Letter from Mayme Sullivan of Denver and others.

AUG 4 1943

Married Pte. Lesveque in Littlehampton. Sergeants beat us in softball—first time.

AUG 8 1943

A glider just flew over our house, pulled by a massive four engine bomber.

AUG 15 (midnight) 1943

Awakened early by gunfire. All up on the roof to see a great battle of ack ack. Windows shake when bombs fell, possibly at Portsmouth or Chichester. Where no fires were seen, we could see smoke in moonlight.

Tracer bullets and search lights looked like New York's World Fair.

AUG 16 1943

Victory! Roll up the map of Sicily. Axis troops evacuate. Lance Corporal J.P. Leaneally Irish Guards, first V.C. awarded in ranks this war. He is from Tipperary, neutral Eire. Is it neutral? First V.C. of war among officers won by another Irishman.

AUG 17 1943

Essex Scottish Pipers are in camp across road and wake us up with the strains of Johnny Copeland. I am scribbling this in back of Joe Grant's truck. No table, no chair, no nothing.

AUG 24 1943

Started long maneuvers. Marched four miles to Chichester with pack, web, etc., then four more miles at end of journey to bush between Southampton and Winchester at Hiltenbury Camp.12 inches between cots, therefore one must be sober to dress. Lots of rain but our tents good.

Essex piper Archie Beaton playing his trademark left-handed pipes.

AUG 25 1943

Church in village too small as we came to Mass, so I said Mass outside for 300 men, put suitcase on post for an altar. Next Mass at Stoneham camp for armoured division R.C.L.I and R.C.E. etc.

AUG 27 1943

Southampton is half in ruins but docks functioning. Winchester Cathedral
is majestic and stately. British cooks are feeding us now. The lads say they
are starving. Canadian cooks are better.
Shower baths are first since march here- worth a million- almost.
We wash our own cutlery and care for it.
I say Mass each morning in the shower room before the shavers arrive.
Louis builds up empty petrol cans for an altar.

AUG 27 1943

Padre hour going on as usual in the mess tents. Catholic Digest has good articles
for discussion. "Our Lord's Sense of Humor" is title of this week's debate. He had
plenty, as evidenced in Scripture. For example, He preached temperance, yet turned
water into wine at Cana, even after all had well drank.

The modest water saw its God and blushed".   R. Crashaw 1613–1649 metaphysical poet England

I wish the sausages would turn into meat when we roll them over.
They are umpteen percent bread or something.

AUG 27 1943

In spite of inconveniences in woods, lads are in good spirits. Ever since yesterday
even the sun cannot penetrate to dry laundry. Scenery is beautiful.

> *"Who comes not hither n'er shall know*
> *How beautiful the world below".*   *Wordsworth*

I have no spot to say office and meditation except by blazing a trail in the woods.

AUG 27 1943

Why do I take the time to write this since I nor anybody else may ever read it again? ANSWER: It keeps me from getting flat, so I can recall the brighter side of life to some blokes at Padre Hour. Sometimes they see only mud and routine and sweat—damp clothes in the morning and tasteless meals and moneyless pockets and no Second Front—no chance of promotion. Bedroll weight was limited so I couldn't bring gramophone with: McCormack, Kreisler and Paderewski. I heard all personally in Detroit. Very well! We'll compose our own. Let's go lads. Out pipe the Pipers.

AUG 29 1943

Went on 13 mile speed march in 2½ hours with Lieutenant Steward Bull. Just a little half morning work to earn a bath.

SEP 2 1943

War will be four years old tomorrow. Four long short years. "Donna nobis Pacem".

SEP 3 1943

Grant us peace.

Allies invade Italy. National Day of Prayer observed. Eider down bed rolls are comfortable on these cold damp nights. Woods are dense with beech, oak, maple, etc. Blackberries and mushrooms abound, so all pick their own extra rations. Shows and movies brought to camp frequently by Y.M.C.A.

SEP 9 1943

Marched through transit area near Southampton to seaport, then to train for home. Some day we'll sail, we hope, beyond the white cliffs of Dover from this port to liberate Europe from Nazism. Some ships go within sight of French coast to draw out enemy fighters, but they don't bite. Neither did their tanks move in France. Millions may go through the same process before the blood bath of Europe is over. Many will never come back. There is something worse than death and that is: "victory of evil".

SEP 19 1943

Three Masses as usual. Attendance increasing since one lad reads Mass in English. Sublime and ancient prayers lend devotion. Since many don't use prayer books, they consequently daydream. Many more communicants of thanksgiving for victory in Italy. The Pope's broadcast got Italy out of the war.

"Believe it or not", on opening of 5th year of total war, I recall that although I carry the Holy Oils of Extreme Unction by special Chaplain privilege, I only used them twice since I was commissioned. The first soldier anointed was 6 ft 2 in. My father had weathered 82 winters. He was first to salute me. This was in Dec 1939. In my years in 'bomby' old England, where thousands were killed, I only anointed one, a Free-Frenchman. Parish priests anointed our lads, all of whom were killed accidentally. This is an unusual record in view of the fact that 230 of my military parish were casualties at Dieppe, but through the fortunes of war I know not how many received the "Last Rites" in French hospitals or German prisons. I thought I had taught our lads to keep out of jail but the majority of the 230 landed there (German prisoners).

SEP 26 1943

Brother Ray's card from Midland just in time. Churchill back from America. Three years ago when a few squadrons of R.A.F. fought off German bombers while we listened and slept Churchill said: *"Never in the field of human conflict was so much owed by so many to so few."*

I quoted it to men- referring to frequent communicants on Sundays. Communicants in the Canadian Army are in the minority, but they are the leaven to permeate the Army. Before it is too late there may be a spiritual mobilization proportionate to the spectacular increase in the strength of R.A.F. in last three years.

" Hope springs eternal in the human breast."
Alexander Pope

SEP 27 1943

20th move in England. Always moving! Always moving!

OCT 9 1942

It can be mighty cold at night, this England. Let's put another blanket on. That will make five. Let's put another log on the fire. No!—a punishable offence till November. In war time winter starts with the calendar, not the weather. Coal must be saved. After visiting ruins of London on last leave and talking to civilian heroes, I ran across Churchill's thoughts, which will one day prove to be prophetic, at least for this war.

> *"I see the damage done by enemy attacks; but I see side by side the devastation and amid the ruins, quiet, confident, bright and smiling eyes, beaming with a consciousness of being associated with a cause far higher and wider than any human or personal issue. I see the spirit of an unconquerable people".*

NOV 1 - 5 1943

Cambridge University course of lectures similar to Oxford one year ago. We lived and dined with "Dons" (teachers), an enjoyable leave.

NOV 29 1943

Out to get a spot of air and a walk before bath and a bed. I was gazing up through the fog to find a dog fight, sound of which was clear. Machine guns put up a rattling good show. Siren hadn't sounded. When I heard the bullets mow the leaves off the trees a few yards away, I woke up to the fact that I didn't have my steel helmet and had three Masses to say the following morning. As I tore for the house, a bomb dropped several miles away from another plane, I suppose, or perhaps from the one over me.

DEC 16 1943

Wow! A whole month gone and nothing reported in Diary. Reason—too busy making history to record it. Blank days of this hatch-patch Diary are often most important but not recorded.

DEC 16 1943

During first few weeks of December 2nd Division Chaplains came to our 4th Brigade Units in packs, similar to Hitler's submarines. Results—best yet in preparation for our 4th Christmas at war and 5th since the beginning. Thus when the romance of 3½ years in England is naturally ebbing out from a natural point of view, the "Divine Romance" can take precedence and hold our attention, if we jockey into position beneath the salutary rays of light of Him who gives song to the birds and beauty to the English Landscape. From Studdert Kennedy, Anglican Chaplain in last war the following:

"Bread of thy body give me for the fighting.
Give me to drink Thy Sacred Blood for wine.
While there are wrongs that need me for the righting,
While there is warfare splendid and divine."

Mild flu is racing over fortress island home. It carries away about 700 weekly to cemeteries but they are mostly over 55 and therefore not military age. They are scrapping with the same pest in Germany and not being so victorious. Christmas mail and parcels coming in, best yet, from those keeping the home fires burning.

DEC 16 1943

I said Mass in private Chapel of Hillaire Belloc, foremost Catholic historian and Chivalrous knight of God and Country. Alone in the Chapel I picked up his prayer book and found a clipping of the following quaint and provocative inscription on an ancient stone slab in Cathedral of Lubec Germany:

"Thus speaketh Christ our Lord to us:
Ye call Me Master and obey Me not
Ye call Me Light and see Me not
Ye call Me Walk and walk Me not
Ye call Me Wise and follow Me not
Ye call Me Fair and love Me not
Ye call Me Rich and ask Me not
Ye call Me Eternal and seek Me not
Ye call Me Gracious and trust Me not
Ye call Me Noble and serve Me not
Ye call Me Just and fear Me not
If I condemn you blame me not."

Some good has come out of Germany even in the midst of total war. It's up to us to put more good back into Germany when they wave the white flag.

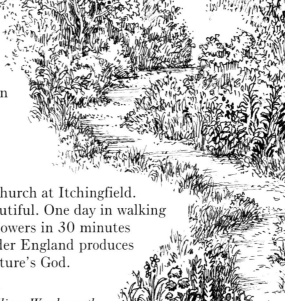

DEC 19 1943

4 o'clock—visited ancient 12th century church at Itchingfield. Tea with Anglican Vicar. Gardens are beautiful. One day in walking through bush, he picked 29 varieties of flowers in 30 minutes without stepping from the path. No wonder England produces Wordsworths who rose from nature to Nature's God.

"Who comes not hither n'er shall know
how beautiful the world below" William Wordsworth

"What is life—if full of care, we have
not time to stand and stare." William Henry Davis

Helping 2nd Division Padres to hear Confessions at Horsham, Brighton, Worthing and camps in the area. At the end of busy days which resolve into busy weeks and months and years-my 5th Christmas at war, humble military curtainless, carpetless, undecorated billets and collapsible cots, are as welcome as civilized sleeping bags and palaces of Kings.

Christmas Day 1943

MIDNIGHT- To Deanne Park Mission in huts near Horsham. Father Leblanc from St Joseph's Oratory Montreal prepared best choir yet and improvised an exquisite altar, sanctuary light even. I sang High Mass and put lots of incense in and let'er smoke. Several hundred 4th Brigade R.C.A.S.C. and R. Regiment C., one truck load of Essex Scottish, and some of 4th F.D.S. Mr. and Mrs. Jebb attended with Mary Anne. She is the daughter of Hillaire Belloc. They also brought Robert Spraight, famous English convert and radio actor and broadcaster for B.B.C. He had lectured at Assumption College Windsor, in Ontario.

Men say it was the most solemn Christmas in peace or war. All but half a dozen waited for the second Mass. The French choir glued them to their benches.

2:30 a.m.- after traveling home five miles I hit the hay. At 9:00 a.m. seven miles away I said Mass at R.H.L.I. 10:30 a.m.- heard Confessions at beautiful Horsham Church. 12 noon Mass at Essex Scottish- five miles to huts. All Masses were in huts in the mud, in the woods but they were all better than the stable at Bethlehem. 3:00 p.m. Christmas dinner as good as any in Canada. It was my first and only meal this 1943 Christmas Day.

DEC 31 1943

All out to New Year's Eve party but Captain of Glengarry Highlanders and myself. We discussed the international situation and agreed on most points until he told me that a Pope in the middle ages made a pronouncement that a woman didn't have a soul. At least he recognizes that there is a soul, so we had something in common.

NEW YEAR'S DAY 1944.   This is the year, God bless 1944.

I had three Masses as usual, all in improvised altars in camps, so had a good appetite for turkey at noon. Lads sobered up (almost) from the eve's jollifications. General Burns and several dozen officers accepted the invitation to call and have some short ones during the afternoon. As we commence our 5th chilly winter in England we are cheered by the fact that this is the year. The lads are anxious to get it over with and get back. There are no fatalists, but this year they'll deliver the goods or die in the attempt. They've now got the tools to finish the job. There will be no unemployment in the "Fortress Europe" soon.

JAN 2 1944

We never knew we would be so long in the land of flowers and song and bombs. You never miss the well till the water goes dry. The sweet strains of "O Salutaris & Tantum Ergo", the incense ascending like a prayer, crowned with the blessing has a relaxing effect on body as well as soul. Try it all ye who scan these rambling lines.

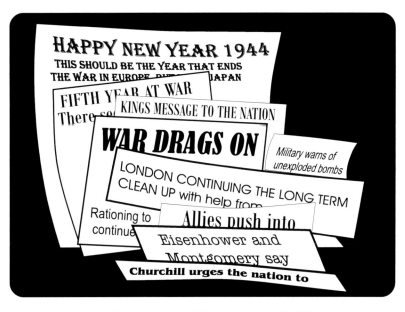

HAPPY NEW YEAR 1944
THIS SHOULD BE THE YEAR THAT ENDS THE WAR IN EUROPE ... JAPAN

FIFTH YEAR AT WAR
There ...

KINGS MESSAGE TO THE NATION

WAR DRAGS ON

Military warns of unexploded bombs

LONDON CONTINUING THE LONG TERM CLEAN UP with help from

Rationing to continue

Allies push into

Eisenhower and Montgomery say

Churchill urges the nation to

JAN 30 – FEB 3 1944

On leave in Scilly Isle 30 miles off Cornwall. Bathed in warm gulf stream. Daffodils, narcissus and flowers galore. Tresco is a tropical garden of palms, etc. Rode in motor launch that picks up R.A.F. in channel. Went through a Sunderland flying boat, the biggest thing that flies. I was the only priest on the isle so had Mass for military and civilians. Farmers were planting potatoes. Many were seasick on small boat going from mainland. I flew back in a twin motor eight passenger Rapede. Cornwall like south Eire- small fields, huts, stone fences. Spring flowers peeping up in England earlier than usual.

FEB 10 1944

Chaplain's meeting at Brighton. Sea breezes cold but it's good to get the tang of the salt air. We enjoyed it for several months in Rye, St. Leonards, Brighton and Middleton in past years. I landed in jail today to visit a soldier who shot another soldier dead in a drunken scrap over a piece of bread. Called at 2nd Division to see Colonel Larry Deziel.

FEB 13 1944

Another show at Victoria Station London. Going for the 9:18 p.m. train home when the guns began to bark. The Germans were above us. Shall I go to shelter or have a spot of tea in Buffet? It was bitterly cold. (The tea was good.) People dined and talked in spite of air attack, and not the big percentage were seen going underground for safety. British calm.

FEB 21 1944

3 a.m. two bombs miles away wake some. My windows rattle. This is too early for Reveille in any man's war so I stay under the blankets. London is getting it hard after months of respite. Snow the second time this winter but not enough to bury flowers.

FEB 28 1944

Well do I remember one year ago today on "Exercise Elm" sleeping on the frozen sod beside the jeep in a wind swept field. It didn't do any harm- just thought it did. Night traveling in jeep with out side curtains made me think of our 1916 Ford with curtains as a luxury. War throws comforts back 30 years.

MAR 1 1944   General Montgomery visits 4th Brigade.

10 a.m. at Christ Hospital Grounds—a memorable day—General Bernard Montgomery who chased the Germans thousands of miles into the sea (not all ¼ million captured) inspects the 4th Brigade. About 2000 were present on parade.

> In passing he stopped and asked me how long I had been with the Brigade.
> "From the beginning" I replied.
> The General: "Oh you must know them all well."

It happened I was the only officer left in Brigade original staff organized in Camp Borden Canada. Montgomery said the appearance of men gave him confidence for future battles and asked for some confidence in him now that we had met and become acquainted. Carry on Monty and we'll back you up. In the cause of freedom everywhere, we'll go as far as he who goes the farthest. We gave him three rousing cheers and on he went.

MAR 9 1944 – Gentlemen—the King

Scene: Old Roman road Billinghurst to London. King George VI inspects 2nd Division. What a sight. Thousands of men, as far as the human eye can see, in both directions- men lined the road side six deep on both sides.

The King walked down the middle wearing a British warmer. Brigadier Lett stopped and told him I was M.B.E.

He asked me if I got it at Dieppe.
I replied: "Soon after sir, from you."

It was bitter cold. We marched ten miles round trip and stood 2½ hours without overcoats, but not without our King.

APR 15 1944

Past two years scribbling in diary will now be chucked in my trunks. Trunks will be stored. We now travel light, but will strike heavy when seas are crossed.

APR 17 1944—False alarm

Move was to a new location not the Old World. Louis and I load the jeep chuck full and start for Dover via Rye. Six miles north of Dover we find Dane Court at Tilmanstone. Bell tent is my office and private Chapel, as at Camp Borden. Area here was once ruled over by pagan king Ethelred. Dover and Folkstone are badly battered by shells from France. On a clear day with glasses one can see the coast of France—traffic on streets 27 miles from enemy. The channel is 21 miles across and we are about six miles back. They can't break the glass of my house (tent).

APR 17 1944

There are fewer hedges here so we see beauty and green fields which were once ruled over by that King Ethelred, converted by St. Augustus in early 7th Century. Canterbury again eight miles north. Marvelous cathedral built on walls of Augustine over 500 feet long, longest crypt in Europe. St. Augustine's Monastery ruins were built on pagan temple of King of Kent 600 A.D. We went to Canterbury on an old Roman road where pilgrims used to travel to the tomb of St. Thomas à Becket, murdered by Knights of King Henry II. The spot near the altar where he fell is marked. Henry came back to do penance.

Canterbury Cathedral

APR 17 1944

Sleeping out. Orchestra of birds wake you up, along with an orchestra of bombers going to work and coming back; busy as bees.

APR 17 1944

Then I would say of the orchestra of birds what an English Poet (Browning I think) said of the thrush, in: "Home—Thoughts, From Abroad":

> *"He sings each song twice over,*
> *Lest you should think he could never recapture*
> *The first fine careless rapture!"*

APR 23 1944

10:30 a.m. Mass. Over 200 gather round altar in field in a complete circle as in Father Coughlin's Church in Detroit. Lieutenant Bud Lynch read the Mass prayers in English and led in dialogue Mass through the loud speaker which I also used as gospel. I heard confessions after Mass till 12:30 p.m. giving communion to 50 who had not been to confession before Mass.

EVENING

Benediction in Dover in Church shelled last week. Twenty miles across channel. France could be seen with naked eye as air was clear. Next time we'll bring field glasses and see traffic on streets near Calais, they say, I have me doubts. We now keep a vigilant ear tuned for a new kind of warning. The siren indicating that shells are coming from France is different from air-raid warnings of the past four years.

Flash of guns can be seen in France. One has 70 seconds to duck into a fox hole. Sight travels quicker than shells. We saw the huge guns that shell back at enemy convoys and French towns. They say that instantly you duck on seeing men in France through glasses. (First sight of enemy I suppose).

APRIL 25 1944   near **Deal in Kent**

Walked four miles half a mile underground in coal mine. Crawled on hands and knees several yards in sweat and heat to see men in shorts hueing next winter's coal. At about 55 a miner is washed out, I mean his lungs are plugged out (I'll turn off the light more frequently in empty rooms to save the underground armies ammunition). Some kids 18 years old don't look so good. Oh! To be born a farmer. They earn their 17 shillings a day. They work all through their evening of life during the sunlight and often until the dark- not even a pension. Those who turn on the heat are turned into the cold selfish world.

"Man's inhumanity to man makes countless thousands mourn".   *Robert Burns*

Deal: Caesar landed here with his Roman legions in 55 A.D.
Dover: They would like to attract visitors but they can only say: "Caesar
          would like to have landed here but the Doverites wouldn't let him".

APRIL 27 1944 – "Invasion"

Now almost complete. A bloodless invasion of birds from North and South Africa and from Europe. Others will come later when flies and bees are almost fat enough for a bird's ration. Millions spend a few months here when their hometown is too hot.

MAY 4 1944

Watch arrives from brother Walt. "Well timed" on eve of my birthday. Cooks bake up an excellent cake. I don't ask them where they got the ingredients. Louis has a good memory. I forgot my birthday until cake appeared. On the wrong side of 40, one likes to skip a birthday, especially as many over 40 are sent home.

MAY 5 1944

Left early for Scunthorpe in Lincolnshire for special training in storm boats on River Trent. We are sleeping out for two weeks. Froze (almost) last night till we moved to a cluster of bushes. Say daily Mass outside when no tent is available at 4:45 a.m. When a good spring day comes we forget rain and cold.

MAY 18 1944

Letter from George—not George VI this time but my nephew George (Dalton) O'Connor sergeant in R.C.A.F. just arrived at the Front.

MAY 23 1944

All trunks and surplus kit to be shipped to Aldershot and stored for duration of war. I must now debate what to take and what not to. This is the first time I will be separated from trunks in four years, except a few weeks of maneuvers now and then. This is possibly the last entry in this hatch-patch diary and perhaps the last diary of any kind.

It looks as if... "this is it" Amen

I have told Quartermaster to send my three trunks containing valuable clothes, photos and souvenirs home. I have no debts. Insurance was paid up to date this year at Confederation Life in Windsor. My will is at the McEwan & Knox Law Firm in Windsor. I have quite a substantial bank account at Bank of Montreal London England which I was saving for a trip to Rome and Lourdes (after a business trip to Berlin).

MAY 28 1944   Pentecost Sunday **Tilmanstone near Dover**

"Veni Sancti Spiritum" (Come Holy Spirit)

Big doings today make news for opening of this record of events in uncertain days of the future. Col. Mike O'Neil, Senior Chaplain Overseas spoke to all 2nd Division who could get off duty to attend Mass. About 4500 in five locations. I have a Bell tent and am sole proprietor. I have bed, table to say Mass, clay floor, no windows to break, no door to slam.

MAY 29 1944

Within 22 miles of the enemy off Dover, General Dwight D. Eisenhower, four star General and chief of Allied Armies of Liberation inspected 4th Bde. Hurriedly he ran the gauntlet among thousands, occasionally talking to some, mostly privates. Brigadier Lett introduced him to me.

He inquired whether I had a hard time controlling the lads and with a few "Yes sirs", I convinced him that they were OK.
(what else could I say?) I was surrounded. We have the drop on Ike. What chance has he of promotion?

JUN 1 1944
Living on a Millionaire's Estate:

Lowell, you are right but the millionaire on whose estate we now live has a distorted sense of humor. Guinea hens night and day interrupt so much you can't hear your watch.

"And what is so rare as a day in June?
Then, if ever, come perfect days...
Whether we look, or whether we listen,
We hear life murmur, or see it glisten;"

James Russell Lowell

JUN 3 1944

Vehicles are immobilized for making waterproof, that is, they can now go through water up to your neck.

JUN 4 1944

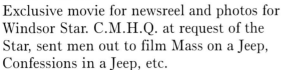

Exclusive movie for newsreel and photos for Windsor Star. C.M.H.Q. at request of the Star, sent men out to film Mass on a Jeep, Confessions in a Jeep, etc.

To the skill of Tommy Burns on the Pipes, over 200 men of war marched in, in stately formation. I encouraged them (with success) to be non-regimental, to crowd around this 20th Century Jeep altar on wheels, to be close to the invigorating "Bread of Life" as did the Christians of early Rome. Hosts had to be covered to avoid wind.

JUN 6 1944 – D-DAY – 4 a.m. – LIBERTY–PEACE–HAPPINESS

I was glad crows and Guinea hens woke me for I heard a continual roar of Bombers going to work. It was near noon when I heard they were the advance guard of Invasion. We are not only living in the presence of History, we are makers of History. Forces of liberation landed in France. We are only 26 miles away and will go soon perhaps. Everybody cheered up, looking at maps. Traded in Jeep on motor wagon, which I call "Mobile Bungalow". Lou and I are busy with hammer and saw building in boxes for clothes, books. We prefer it to Jeep because winter might come and we have oil stove.

JUN 15 194

Bang! Dover shelled. Seventeen killed. Many wounded. General Foulkes, 2nd Division invited me to supper and a party at Bde. H.Q. At midnight we heard battle and saw some Pilotless planes. Again, we are living in the presence of History. No one is unduly disturbed. Hundreds going to Mass and Communion daily.

JUN 22 1944

With Mass kit on my back haversack, I rode on rear of motorcycle to Essex Scottish. Walked home that evening, seven miles with pack.

JUN 24 1944

Bang! Dover shelled again.

JUN 27 1944

While on Route March a pilotless plane winged overhead. They are being shot down all around us, some in channel. Some do damage. Four hundred in 4th Bd. units received Communion last week at morning and evening Masses. I am now learning the "General Absolution" in the plural.

JUN 30 1944 - AT LAST

At 2:30 in morning start for port of Embarkation. Two days in martialing area then to one of U. S. Liberty Ships (56 days to make). Lived on sea several days until convoy assembled; slept (almost) in a box in the hold—3rd bunk up—it was OK—didn't fall out. Had Mass amongst the ropes. Carried Mass kit on back with week's change of clothes.

JUL 5 1944

This is D-Day for 4th Bde. Pleasant trip, anchored a few miles from French coast among thousands of ships. Hated to go to bed way down in hot spot of ship. Dreaming of Liberty Ships, 4000 in all I think- -all makes, big and small on D-Day.

JUL 7 1944- Invasion Beach of Juno on June 6 at La Valette

Small craft took us in. Ships as far as the eye could see. Waited for tide to go out and walked in from the boats- onto the beach purpled with noble blood of Canadian and Allied assault one month ago.

Ruins of German fortifications all around us. Talked to French peasant lady with wooden shoes. She smiled approval of our liberating Normandy. Some didn't. Not a house on seaside villa undamaged. 500 bombers attack Germans 12 miles away at Caen. There was a sight, saw three bombers crash and five men bail out. At midnight we move towards the front near Caen.

JUL 8 1944

First official act yesterday on French soil was to put "Ave Maria" on gramophone. Also John McCormack singing "Say a Little Prayer". John answered my letter when I told him this. The continued thunder all day is artillery. No one is alarmed. All are anxious to do their duty to God and country, After Mass 500 men sang "God Save The King" and "Oh Canada". In liberated France it was a thrill!

JUL 9 1944   Padre's first announcement in liberated France

From: H.Q. 4th Cdn. Inf. Bde.

1. There is an old religious custom older than the Christian Church to offer prayers and sacrifice for those fallen in battle.

2. On Monday July 10 at 0800 hrs. There will be a REQUIEM MASS and communion at R.C. Church BAZENVILLE for all allied manhood who purpled the beaches of Normandy with their noble blood.

3. Even though duties may prevent parades to the church, all soldiers of good will, will expect all officers of good will to announce this.

4. 500 4th Bde. men of war and their Chaplain who received Communion today on their first Sunday in France will always remember with loyalty the units who encouraged them to attend, as a thanksgiving offering for their safe arrival. The good news will resound throughout Normandy.

M. J. Dalton, Major.

JUL 11 1944
To Verson (a hot spot near Caen)- up to the Front at night.

FIRST TASTE OF TOTAL WAR <u>by sight</u>
from massive flashes
of Artillery.

SECOND TASTE OF TOTAL WAR <u>by smell</u>
of dead soldiers and livestock. Days in the sun was a feast for maggots.
I am not a good smeller but the smell of human flesh is depressing.

JUL 11 1944

THIRD TASTE OF TOTAL WAR <u>by sound</u>
from moaning minnies that scatter
shrapnel everywhere.

FOURTH TASTE OF TOTAL WAR <u>surrounded by soil,</u>
as all are dug in now, even the high priced warriors. Buck privates can teach
me a few tricks on digging in. All are their own architects and contractors.

JUL 12 1944

Move to Casualty Clearing Post—0900 hrs—terrific mortar fire blasts fell like hail in our orchard. One piece came in the back door of my truck and out the side one foot from where my feet were. I was too busy to be unduly alarmed as I rushed out to help a dying British Ack Ack gunner to recite: "Jesus mercy".

I am now veteran enough to move into a slit trench even though it is too noisy to sleep, it's better than above ground. I got to sleep at 3 a.m. The first sleep in three nights. Our own artillery keeps us all awake.

First funeral in France—Donnelly, whose jeep got a direct hit as we were in convoy to front. Units are ahead of Bde. H.Q. therefore more casualties. I moved to 11th Fd. Amb. to help gallant 4th Bde. as a lot were wounded jeeping back. German mortar fire keeps us close to trenches where we sleep.

Back cross roads shelled as my driver Louis and I were approaching. A Fd Gun got a direct hit about 20 yards from us. Funerals everyday now on side of road. Soldiers will be moved to a cemetery as soon as shell fire is beyond range.

JUL 13 1944

Advanced dressing Station near Caen. Three non-Catholic stretcher bearers, McGregor, Bond and Quigley pray the "Our Father" with me in a trench. In spite of intense Artillery fire and shrapnel falling all around, one of them had to go out before dawn and pick up some wounded, and he did it.

JUL 17 1944

Bombs, mortars, machine guns, all plaster us in our wee orchard dugouts. All vehicles and ambulances pierced, tires etc. Shrapnel cut a limb off a tree over my head while I was in the trench and pierced my hat which was on the ground above. Dust storm raised by shrapnel terrific, all week under mortar fire. Three Bde. officers and eight men were hit.

JUL 18 1944

To front in an armored car—back in jeep—tripped over enemy and allied dead. Often went back to Bde. H.Q. from C.P.C. with Mass kit on my back. My haversack was formerly used by a Jewish soldier Dave Croll of Windsor Essex Scottish.

JUL 18 1944

Essex Scottish held the line under mortar fire for over a week without gain of ground but prestige galore. Tank and artillery support failed since radio knocked out. I visited the remnant tired and weary.

JUL 18 (later) 1944

Louvigny. This "Holding Area" designated by Montgomery to be just that—"to hold like a puppy to a root". In this town a happy smiling Lieut. Wm. Patterson brought us Lieut. Bud Lynch, saying to me "Padre look after Bud he has a bad wound". Bud, with a mangled arm brought back prisoners. He often read the Mass in English for me. Bud said: "Rub my hand Padre", but the circulation was failing and he was jeeped to field hospital and his arm was amputated.

Editor's note– Later as a hockey broadcaster Bud and Red Wing Hockey in Detroit were synonymous.

Dave Croll became mayor of Windsor and the first Jewish Canadian Senator.

JUL 19 (later) 1944

"My God it's Patterson". I could tell by the pale face in the jeep that he was dead. I was refused permission to visit the men at the front. Then I said to the Military Police: "Patterson's brother is the Adjutant to the Colonel in R.Reg.C. May I go up and tell him his young brother is dead?" He gave me an armored car and chauffeur and I found Adjutant Patterson sitting on the grass checking up on the casualties (no place else to do it).When I told him the sad news, he cried and said:"I promised our parents I would look after him".

JUL 19 (later) 1944

Anglican Chaplain Harold Appleyard was at prayer—Last Rites in biggest mass burial I saw since Dieppe. Canadians and Germans—dozens of them in the sun. Here as in the ruins of Liseaux, **human flesh smell is depressing.**
The future Bishop Appleyard came back with Patterson and me when I asked him to bury Patterson's brother. I shouldn't have asked him for he was exhausted, but calm.

Editor's note. At Verrieres Ridge On July 20 1944, the Essex Scottish was decimated for the second time after Dieppe. With 244 men dead, wounded or missing the Regiment ultimately suffered the most casualties of any Canadian Regiment in the entire war.

JUL 22-23 1944

All come to Mass and Communion in a damp cold cave inhabited by evacuees of Caen. (30 ft. under rock) French sang beautifully. Mass again in caves at Fleury-sur-Orne. Later, I heard there was a War Correspondent attending, but I did not meet him.

JUL 24 1944 *From a newspaper report by Maurice Dejardins—to the Canadian Press*
The Padre included this material in his Diary Supplement

ONE THRILL PACKED HOUR IN BATTLE BEYOND CAEN
A DRAMATIST'S DREAM

Three neutralize live mortar shell
Padre conducts Service in underground Grotto

This is a factual report of what happened in a thrill packed hour in this village on the mossy banks of the Orne River just south of Caen, though it sounds more like the Mad Dream of a Hollywood script writer.

It's an epic complete with sound and its scenario contains enough episodes for at least six old time movie thrillers.

Here's what could be seen and heard, during those action jammed 60 minutes.

1. **A British Tank Force** attacking and recapturing the village of Maltot across the Orne to the west.

2. **A Canadian Infantry Push** in the rich wheat fields towards Verrieres to the southeast.

3. **A Cordon of our Big Guns** just outside Fleury hammering enemy positions with ear-splitting ferocity.

4. **German Shells** landing in the Orne River forcing French refugees who were watching the tank show to scamper inside the deep quarries where they had lived since D-Day June 6.

5. **A Sergeant-Royal Canadian Engineers** helping two R.A.F. bomb removal experts disengage an unexploded mortar shell from a rubble pile.

6. **A Canadian Padre** saying Mass for soldiers and civilians in a dark Grotto under the only Brewery in the Calvados department of France.

Editor's note: further written material
from Maurice Dejardins.

1. The **British Tank Force**

We could see the tanks firing as they advanced through smoke and bursting enemy shells. Among the crowd watching was a blonde partisan girl in the uniform of a second lieutenant of the Fighting French, who came to the quarries to distribute soap to the civilians.

2. The **Canadian Infantry Push**

We talked to mud-caked infantrymen who pointed to the flat plains saying: "There's our battlefield and all hell's breaking. Our slit trenches are full of water and mortar shells are falling everywhere".

3. The **Cordon of our Big Guns.**

One didn't need binoculars to see farms, which our battalions recaptured and were defending successfully against armored onslaughts. We left the observation posts when conversation became impossible due to our own artillery barrage.

4. The **German Shelling**

The shells were landing in the Orne River and crashing at our feet, so we all did the logical thing and ran into the nearest grotto. But the French girl stayed a few minutes watching the shells burst.

5. The **Sgt. Robert J. King Winnipeg R.C.E.**

King said he was helping the men in the dangerous job of lifting an unexploded mortar shell from the debris of a house because they helped him earlier in the day in his specialty-
defusing German teller mines.

6. The **Canadian Padre Maj. M. Dalton-Essex Scottish**

The Padre from Windsor Ontario, was celebrating Mass to the accompaniment of the frail voices of French children singing Latin hymns. Three carbide lamps provided the dim lighting and you could hardly distinguish the altar from the entrance near which a refugee was getting a haircut from a civilian barber. In the narrow passageway leading to the underground, we saw a TRI-COLOR FLAG which had been assembled the morning the Canadians took Fleury. Flag was made from a gardener's blue apron, a woman's slip, and a red bandana handkerchief.

JUL 24 1944

I remained with 21 F.D.S. a few days and nights in the cave. Dampness in cave has been here since William the Conqueror, soon after 1066, hued out stone for the great Cathedrals of England. 300 casualties came through in nine hours during fierce night battle. I helped stretcher bearers carry them from jeeps. Buried several within. Many died from shrapnel fire. My name was printed on a little white cross, by error. Pall bearers ducked once but recovered their balance.

JUL 25 1944

A wicked night. While saying vespers at midnight bombing commenced. I was in my truck- it was pierced- only a few minor casualties but many trucks burned close by. I returned to sick bay to assist in rush from the front. Father Larame and Henshaw were there to help bury Germans.

JUL 25 1944

At one Mass I turned to give last blessing and not one soldier was in sight. They all had ducked into the trenches.

JUL 26 1944

Mass in mill surrounded by tons of wheat. So far I have not had to interrupt Mass due to shelling, but plenty heard close by. The Mass brings at least ½ hour respite from mortar fire. Earlier at a Mass I broke the rule of "No collections at Mass". The lads gave thousands of francs. The Pastor was joyful. I should have asked for a second collection.

Awakened at 6 o'clock to bury a dead German. (They assured me he was dead).

I went to a majestic German tank they had towed back. I said "Produce your corpse". They couldn't. His feet were locked at the controls—they asked for a saw.

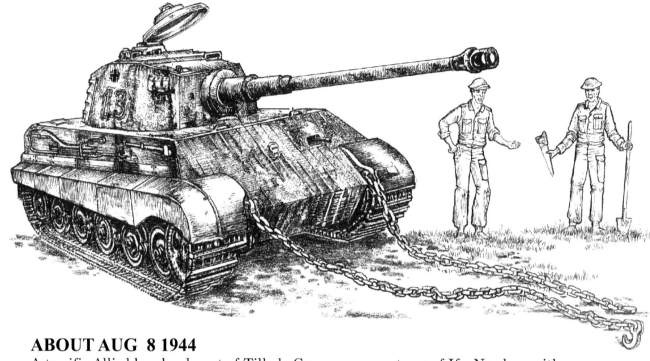

ABOUT AUG 8 1944

A terrific Allied bombardment of Tilly la Campagne near town of Ifs. No sleep with that stuff breaking. Buried four unknown soldiers burnt in trucks—direct hit. Advance is steady but yard by yard gained at human sacrifice. Almost everyday I see some old friends coming through Dressing Stations, who may not see the light of morrow.

ABOUT AUG 8 1944

Many German prisoners now flowing back, some wounded, some too young
to shave. Some Poles and Austrians. They have had enough, a close shave.

Dust worse than London fog- many towns totally destroyed, excellent crops ruined.
Goggles needed. Clipped off all my hair- can't clean your hair- due to dust, which
sweat holds on.

AUG 15 1944

To Bayeux Canadian Hospital.
Many wayside Calvaries in France. On one I read:"Spes Unica" (the Only Hope). Out
of this crucifixion of France will come a resurrection. Their only salvation is through
suffering. Louis and I pulled into an orchard where a bomb had dropped and hit the
place where our truck was parked before. Three F.D.S. killed and eight injured nearby.

AUG 17 1944

On move again through Bretteville towards Falaise. Rocquancourt a mess. Allied gap closing south of Falaise. Germans outwarred again. Found church not too badly shelled. Louis will clear broken masonry off what was a beautiful altar, and men will attend Mass amid the ruins. Sometimes I hide chalices from looting sacrilegious soldiers.

AUG 17 1944

Too busy making history to scribble about it for the rest of this memorable month. One midnight plunge brought 2nd division clear of hills to open country. Let's cross the Seine. We passed hundreds of burned out tanks and vehicles on German retreat route. They dug in again at Elbeuf on the banks of the Seine—a costly week for both sides. Then we crossed the Seine in high gear.

AUG 17 1944

We passed historic Rouen, world famous
Cathedral from whence LaSalle set out in
1667 to explore Mississippi. Joan d'Arc
was burnt at the stake here.
German prisoners on road everywhere.

*Illustration based on a photograph
of 2nd Canadian Infantry Division
moving through Rouen
photo by Harold G Aikman.*

SATURDAY SEPTEMBER 2 1944 – DIEPPE "At long last"

I said Mass at Cdn. Cemetery where 854 allied lie buried since August 19 1942. All
Regiments of Bde. attended and received Communion as they knelt on graves of their fallen
comrades. Many old friends' graves were recognized. 539 Essex Scottish, including 28 officers
attacked Dieppe. 44 returned—no officers. That was when I was made Colonel for a day.

SEP 2 1944 – DIEPPE – Afternoon

To beaches to meditate on sublime thought immortalized by Father Hill.

> *"The Battlefield is often holy ground to the Chaplain,*
> *For he is treading on soil soaked with the blood of men,*
> *Who have kept their vow of obedience to duty even*
> *unto death.*
> *It is this solemn thought which dispels the horror of*
> *scenes of concentrated slaughter.*
> *The imagination lifts this carnage up onto the altar of*
> *Sacrifice and a Battlefield is seen in the light of Calvary".*

Germans were dug in under tons of rock. Their food stores were still burning.
They destroyed almost all as they left.

SEP 3 1944   Day of National Prayer, Mass on bones of "Risen Soldiers".

War five years old today but our 2nd Division is five years younger. I said three
Masses, the last two in the Dieppe Canadian Cemetery. General Crerar spoke.
Newsreels were clicking to preserve for the world the story of liberation of Dieppe.

Afternoon

Thousands of 2nd Div. marched through town. Thousands of French lined the roads
for miles to welcome their liberators.

Vive le Canada – Vive le France.

SEP 5 1944

I slept in a Dieppe Convent that the Germans had used previously and later returned to
the Sisters. I felt guilty the morning I awoke and learned that I slept in the very bed
that German General Rommel had used for many months during the heat of the War.

SEP 6 1944

On the move again. It was the longest move in France up to St. Omer towards Calais area- night traveling through dense bush in rain, rain, rain. Flying bomb base near bush captured. Line up for dinner in pouring rain. No time to stop for breakfast while enemy are fleeing. This trip led us to another change of money.

SEP 7 1944

Into Belgium to mop up a few enemy near Ostende, near West Kappell, Blankenburg Nieuport etc. People are loud in praise of Canada. Nearly all speak French and Flemish. A great relief to see healthy kids among fertile lands. Crops are excellent but flooded out. Germans departed here just recently- they heard the Canadians coming.

SEP 13 1944

Flanders charming and hospitable—on wheels again across border into France near Dunkirk. Boys are lonesome leaving friendly Belgians. Belgian horses are masterpieces of equine pulchritude and beauty and strength. The lads say the same thing about the women. "Get up, horses is me hobby"said I to the lad who said to his two minute acquaintance: "we'll have to make love fast. We only have a short stay". Some are serious and want to get married. I saved a few marriages.

One lad handed me a photo of his girl. I said: "I asked for a photo of your girl". He said: "That's it". Says I: "Are you going to look at that face over the breakfast table for 50 years? Her legs are beautiful, but they will be under the table". He didn't marry, didn't even ask for the photo back.

SEP 13 1944

Big guns heard shelling Dunkirk. I guess we're in for a scrap. We traverse roads where almost ½ million B.E.F. fled to Dunkirk beaches in 1940 in valiant fight for liberty.

"O earth what changes thou hast seen." Tennyson

SEP 14 1944

Mass in church with soul-stirring Plain-Chant by refugees of Dunkirk. People load us down with fruit etc. as in Belgium. Big battle here in 1940. Several dozen English and German buried here. It is hot enough for a sun bath these days but I'm too busy writing next of kin letters.

SEP 16 1944

Passed over the Battlefield where Father Will Doyle S.J. Chaplain was killed near Ypres in 1918. Monument there also for Canadian dead.

SEP 16 1944

Back to Antwerp, Belgium a most charming city, stately buildings and hospitable people. All, even children, say "Good Morning" and shower cars with fruit and flowers. Men are holding at Albert Canal. Casualties are light, but a little of that is a lot.

SEP 22 1944

Visited two Br. Hospitals in Brussels containing Canadians. Met Col. Dave Croll there. As private Croll, he used to salute me. Now I salute him. Visited church of King Albert and the Royal Palace. Couldn't get a meal there but fruit and ice cream for a few Francs.

SEP 25 1944

First swim in Europe indoors, smaller than Lake Huron. To house of Rubens, world famous painter. Jan Van Hercht took me through his ancient house and paint shop.

OCT 4 1944

Said Mass on St. Francis Feast Day at Franciscan Monastery. Lads too busy fighting to go to Mass. My spare time is spent visiting them in hospitals.

OCT 5 1944

Heard Solomon, one of the world's famous pianists play Beethoven's Moonlight Sonata. Beethoven's parents lived at Malines and moved to Germany. A few days visiting hospitals and then on to Capellen five miles from Holland. Shrapnel pierced a school-only one hurt. They teach me the Belgian National anthem, I teach them "O Canada".

Moonlight Sonata

First Movement, Op. 27, No. 2

Ludwig van Beethoven
(1770–1817)

OCT 8 1944

Buried two more Essex Scottish today. Belgians present us as usual with flowers and tears. Belgium people like to hear me sing in Mass: "Oremus pro rege nostro Leopoldo". Their King Leopold is in German prison. *"Let us pray for our King Leopold."*

Crossed border into Holland at Putte in Major Slater's jeep. Did not set foot yet on Holland soil—only reconnaissance. You would not know the International line was crossed if it were not for different colours of flags draping liberated city (red, white and blue). Belgium colours are red, black and orange.

Dutch welcome us as liberators—for driving out foreign tyrant. This is now the 3rd country in which we walked in retreating steps of hated foreign invader.
I sang my first 'High Mass' in liberated Europe. It is refreshing to sing a Mass with much splendor on a beautiful altar after many hurried Masses in dismal, monotonous, devastated scenes of horror. Funerals here have enough pomp and dash to bury a King. Most of them are horse drawn (not ours). The roof and walls of this church are pierced with shell fire, but reparable. Belgium churches are 'Prayerful' churches.

OCT 15 (Sunday) 1944

On to Front for evening Mass. It was scheduled for a beautiful ruined church in Holland but officers condemned it as it was at a crossroads frequently shelled—so we built our collapsible Cathedral in what was left of a once classy house. After Mass I took Communion to mortar platoon at their Front. It's a job finding roads but Louis can do it.

They were huddled in one of few houses left standing, waiting for Germans to commence their nightly attack of brimstone. Communion in the leaky woodshed had more solemnity to it than it would have had in Notre Dame because of: "off to battle soon". Many fertile fields of Holland are flooded by Germans to slow our advance. All around us now guns are opening up, to prevent enemy movement under shield of darkness. If our guns reach them, they can reach us, and so it's time for compline or vespers. *(evening prayer)*

Can anyone read this? Usually written on my knee in a truck—too late to bother setting up my collapsible table. Hence scribbling. Mass near the front, request of Major Joe Picket of Hamilton who won the D.S.O. that morning.

OCT 16 1944

Sergeant Art Charette was an Essex Scottish lad who came to R.H.L.I. during Confession. He told me his platoon couldn't attend Mass as they may have orders to fire anytime. He inquired: "Can you bring Confession to our gun position?" I replied: "If H.Q. will allow it." He was wet, so was I. It was dusk then and it would take us several hours to travel back over strange roads with detours.

I consecrated extra Hosts and started off on foot as H.Q. might stop me if they saw the truck. After some searching and hollering I found them. Their mortar guns appeared in the moonlight temporarily covered from the rain. I stood to hear their Confessions. It was a tense moment as they recited the 'Confiteor' (I confess). Then the prayer of the Roman Centurion to our Lord: "Domine nun sum dignus". (Lord I am not worthy.)

Among some of the men who received Communion, I remember the faces in the light of the oil lamp of Art and of Jim Caba- a youth I had prepared for Confirmation in "Tin Can City" in south Windsor, and a lad Moriarty.

That was Art Charette's last Communion. Next morning a few hours later he fell in honored glory. Do you blame me for by passing H.Q. after such a demand? While he was in England his wife died leaving an infant son. Often at night in Maida Barracks, he would call at my billet and discuss the future of his son and heir. I now have some definite facts to comfort his next of kin.

OCT 17 1944

R.H.L.I. would sooner fight than eat and you ought to see them eat. They were
attacked early this morning. They obtained their objective but with great cost
as usual. It's comforting to know they were prepared."He that eateth my flesh
hath Everlasting Life." There is a war on here in Holland—and it may be
shaping itself with the intensity of Verson and Caen.

German prisoners in Antwerp want to go to Canada. So do we. They're going, we're
not. Germans want to get back to Germany and homes. So do we. Germans are
going to Canada, Canadians are going to Germany. Solution: let's change uniforms.

OCT 18 1944

Flying bombs or rockets are now hitting Antwerp. They hit a Canadian mobile
bath killing several and injuring dozens. Major Jose's moral is: "Don't take a bath".
Visited three hospitals in Antwerp, bringing papers, prayer books etc. I have seen the
ugliness of war in all its ramifications, in surgical wards. Saw damage to Museum
from rocket bombs. Heard a few fall, which is not soothing to war weary patients.

OCT 22 1944

Mass for Essex Scottish in ruins of Convent school. I told men of Art Charette's last Communion. Life, Eternal Life on the eve of death. Art's little white cross could be seen through what used to be a window. Just one of hundreds of parallel cases.

I remained at H.Q. to get more names of men killed. Capt. Watt killed when at supper last night just right next door. I miss two old reliables of H.L.I. Lieut. J.Williamson of Ottawa, whom I married in Littlehampton. His wife's first husband was killed in R.A.F. (I suppose now she'll try the Navy.) Also killed- Sgt. Gendron of Montreal, who used to bring out hidden rations when I dined with C. Company. A direct hit through the roof of their truck was the dead answer. Their driver, in the noise of battle, didn't know they were dead until he got back. When I came out of H.Q. I asked Louis if all that noise was: "theirs coming, or ours going?". Louis said: "That stuff landing on our roof isn't hail".

If I didn't make friends with these gallant lads I'd be a total stranger on a foreign strand. There is one thing worse than this concentrated slaughter, and that is the conquest of evil. Our cause is just "Sursum Corda". *(lift up your hearts)*

> *"I feel it when I sorrow most.*
> *'Tis better to have loved and lost*
> *Than never to have loved at all".*   Tennyson

SPES UNICA —Without a Good Friday—never an Easter Sunday. Mystical Body of Christ is being crucified on the cross of war, but remember: "The Risen Soldier". Best education is at the Front. Sound education in school of experience teaches more in one hour at the Front than my week at Oxford, week at Cambridge, week at sea with British Navy, my years with army, several hours over English channel with R.A.F., or a lifetime in a classroom. At the front, one realizes the littleness of man in spite of monsters of war. We sleep again tonight in the truck. Now another change of currency to guilders.

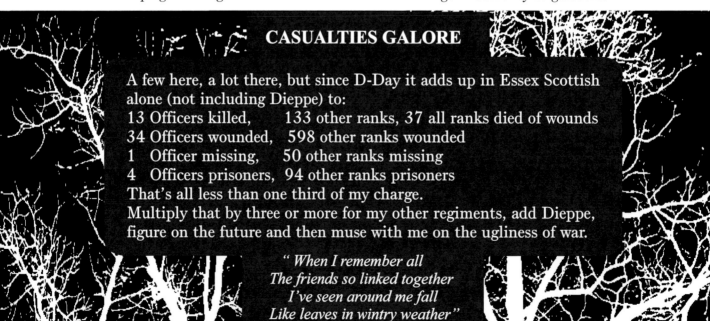

CASUALTIES GALORE

A few here, a lot there, but since D-Day it adds up in Essex Scottish alone (not including Dieppe) to:

13 Officers killed,   133 other ranks, 37 all ranks died of wounds
34 Officers wounded,   598 other ranks wounded
1   Officer missing,   50 other ranks missing
4   Officers prisoners, 94 other ranks prisoners

That's all less than one third of my charge.

Multiply that by three or more for my other regiments, add Dieppe, figure on the future and then muse with me on the ugliness of war.

> *" When I remember all*
> *The friends so linked together*
> *I've seen around me fall*
> *Like leaves in wintry weather"*
> *Thomas Moore*

OCT 26 1944

Often into Holland. Our first night to sleep here in Hoogeriede deserves honorable mention. Lots of wooden shoes, Dutch windmills and shrapnel. Good shooting both ways. All the guns we hear not working for George VI. It's late. Louis and I sleep in the truck again tonight. The enemy made a stand here recently and left ammunition—it's going back to them via air route. Mass tomorrow in bomb plastered Convent Chapel. Protestant lads helped clear debris- windows all broke so it's cold.

OCT 26 1944   HOLLAND

R.Reg.C. to shrapnelled church with hundreds of Hollanders. I heard Confessions during Mass. Curé couldn't chase the Flemish out, they wanted to hear the soldiers' Mass and were edified when almost all arose to receive Communion.

Bless me Father for I have sinned... yeah lots of that...
Padre I can't remember the last time I went to Confession, but yeah, I guess I've sinned. -Sure as hell not proud of some of the things I've done over here. Padre it's been two years since I heard from my wife. I'm not even sure I'll still be a married man when I get home-if I get home. I heard you tell the men you never got married out of consideration for a future Mrs Mike Dalton. You were trying to be funny but you don't have to worry about a woman back home...But Padre that's not all I worry about...I worry that I won't be able to get the ugly things I've seen here out of my mind ...
I wonder how you're gonna get those awful bloody things we've seen out of your mind?

When we brought in that German Tank and you gave me that handsaw, I thought to myself: "I'm a soldier, this is war, I can do this", but I can't get the sight of the dead guy's leg bones out of my mind...sawing through them seemed like nothing at the time, but now I keep seeing them...I'm afraid I'll never get the memory of that out of my mind. I know you saw the dead guy's stumps, and you must have smelled them too, you helped bury him.. How are you going to forget that, or live with that memory?

I remember you telling the guys in Padre hour about the dead men you saw when you were a kid and how it bothered you, until your Church Padre said it was OK to remember, that in time it wouldn't bother you. You know these guys better than anybody; how the hell are they going to live with what they have seen and done?...How am I going to? Some guys can do this soldiering stuff but some can't. They don't talk about it but I know it really bothers some of them. I took a walk a while ago and found a guy I thought I knew out in the bush bawling his head off. I thought he was one of the tough guys. Do you really think in time we can forget anything?

OCT 27 1944

We found what was left of a house- windows without windows, doors without doors, but it's better than sleeping in truck now that fall has struck Holland. Physical training in morning replaces central heating. Two candles enable me to write next of kin. Tony, our Cook, and Bice,were both killed in back yard. I can see their little white crosses from my billet. One small mortar shell got both, while 200 men were within several yards and only two were wounded. Tony Pulas was a Greek Orthodox Catholic, but he figured I was his Chaplain since there are no Orthodox priests in Canadian Army. There are a few Rabbis. Good bye Tony, old timer. You cooked many a good meal for us. Let's hope we'll meet in Heaven.

OCT 29 1944

Machine gunned at night. Ambulance men scurried from their vehicles over wind swept fields in bare feet and blankets. I remained in bed too tired to dodge bullets. No ambulance hit, several killed, dozens were wounded a few hundred yards away.

OCT 30 1944

Goes- that's a nice town which Nazis left without a struggle, leaving choice rations and munitions and clothes. They're short on gasoline. God bless them. Horses pulled big guns. People dress in quaint Dutch costumes. Beautiful stately majestic Churches all around.

HOLLAND – DYKES

Formidable, but when ruptured—behold, fertile fields and crops and roads submerged, but armies of Liberation march on. German ship captured today—a small medical craft.

OCT 1944 FUNERALS IN HOLLAND

Hundreds of Hollanders attend, lay flowers on graves, and make speeches of
thanks to "Risen Soldiers" in the damp earth. I go back to my truck and
tell next of kin that not in vain, did they fall. "Not in vain is your sacrifice".
Halloween, and it looks like it is in town. Cameron Highlanders brought the
pipes, while wounded from the Dykes are frequently stretchered in from miles
away. We saw a few ships warming up in Antwerp. When all 30 miles of dock
are free from enemy fire, Antwerp will take in the stuff to crush the Nazis.

OCT 1944 ALL SAINTS DAY

Whole Brigade on 60 mile trip to Malines, Belgium for a rest, a bath, new clothes
etc. But no rest for the Chaplain. This is his harvest. The Germans having planted
the seed of fear of God in the men, the Regiments are scattered for miles as usual, but
I get to them, Mass morning and evening with an organist, when we can find one.

OCT 1944 ALL SOULS DAY

200 Seminarians chant Libera, etc. in majestic Cathedral. Our clodhoppers are
no longer glued to Holland's Dykes and mud. We are attending Requiem Mass
in probably the most Catholic Country on this dusty planet. Among the world's
greatest scholars and students we catch a fleeting glimpse of early Liturgy of the
Church. Belgium churches and homes are "prayerful," Catholic to the core, not
disunited politically as in France.
60 Catholic Chaplains meet in Antwerp and dined with Cardinal Villaneuve, who
brought us messages from the Pope and from Canada. The thunder of flying bombs
interrupted Col. Roy's introduction. Antwerp has suffered plenty from these
devilish devices. The Cardinal said: "The war must be fought here, not in Canada."

NOV 4–19 1944

Mass for R.Reg.C. now in German concentration camps. Germans burned dozens of
huts and much material as British were one hour on their heels. I had dinner with 11th
Fd. Amb. in parish of Rubens. His original paintings are in the parish church.
Flying bombs pass over frequently. Mass at Malines Cathedral. Battle of Waterloo was a
few miles from Brussels. It was worth seeing. Wellington said: "The Battle of Waterloo
was won on the Playing Fields of Eton College". Napoleon said: "I've had enough."

HOLLAND AGAIN

Rain and mud, but not so much blood this time, not even sweat, it's too cold.
We're near Nijmegen a few miles from Germany. I've slept in truck practically
all the time since our D-Day- when not in the trenches.

NOV 24 1944

It's Cold in the truck. I'll find me a wee room among the ruins from now on,
I hope. Saw gliders broken up. Large American Cemetery here on spot where
900 American Air-Borne troops met their Waterloo, south of Arnhem.

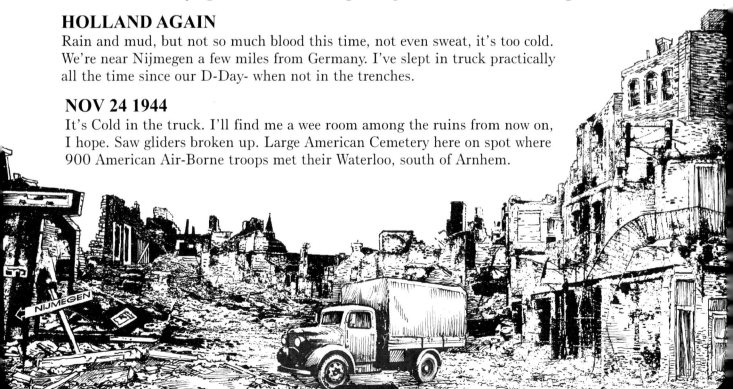

NOV 28 1944

From Msgr. Sheen—his book titled "Friend" arrived. It came at an auspicious moment. I had just descended from an "Observation Post" high up in the Dutch forests to get a squint at Germany (near Berganthal and Kranenburg). The day was clear. German forests looked like ours. Why shouldn't they? The trees are friends. Why shouldn't we be? Only man is goofy. I'll read that book and do my bit. At Nijmegen near Arnhem—stopped in Groesbeck (in ruins) by Provost a few miles from Germany. We're getting there slow but sure.

Joe Sullivan's Maurice got Air Medal and Cluster—killed in air battle—did his bit.

DEC 2 1944

Major Jim Knox B.M. promoted to Sanhurst—Farewell dinner and speeches. Our Regiments back in the trenches, many without any shelter, just dug-outs. Very few got back to Sunday Mass. In ½ hr or less, they were back at the Front. Some of the Regiments now a few hundred yards from the enemy, but concealed by bush. First casualty was a R.Reg.C. lad who was hit by a sniper on his way to dinner. There's a mobile bath at our corner- what a luxury! *Editor's note*

Sanhurst is the British Officer's Training Academy.

DEC 6 1944

Machine gunning not heard so frequently. Last night they were hammering as we used to hear them in movies. It's interesting because I sleep next to a Capt. of Toronto Scottish, in the "Bull Pen". He assures us his valiant lads are shooting in the right direction. We roll over to go to sleep if we can, and he continues talking about the "Vickers Machine Gun" as you would about a new washing machine. That's his business.

DEC 8 1944

Fr. Henshaw said Mass in Amb. Chapel. I heard Confessions. Feast Day of the Assumption, but not much like a big feast Day as most lads are "On Guard" on frontiers of Germany.

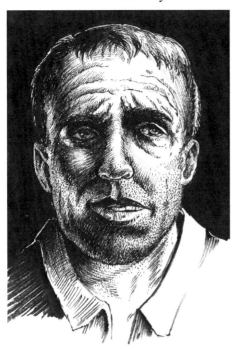

Padre, I'm not Catholic but I've heard you talk and I know you're an educated guy and I think you know that some of us were going to be educated before all this started. Some of us are not as dumb as we look. I finished a year at University—then started reading on my own- then like an idiot I signed up for this. Maybe I really am as dumb as I look!

My folks are really religious. They think God is perfect and makes all things happen for a reason. But Padre they haven't seen what we've seen, or smelled what we've smelled. Yesterday in the dark I stepped on one of those dead bodies we saw—I got blood and guts all over my boots. It soaked right into my skin. I didn't get a chance to wash it off for hours. Now I can't get the smell out of my nose, or is it my mind? I don't know how any of us can ever eat meat again.

If I make it home I don't see how I can tell my folks about this, or about how I sure as hell don't believe in the God they believe in or how any of this can happen for a reason. I know you tell the guys to think of their families and pray, but I can't do either of those things. All I think of is how I can get some more booze.

DEC 9 1944

First snowfall in Holland and plenty rested on our car."I'm dreaming of a white Christmas" while the driver shovels it off. A Holland supper for Civies- 1st Course—about ½ doz. big potatoes, 2nd course – potatoes, 3rd course – apple sauce and brown sour bread (some wheat in it) and ersatz coffee. Patrol post established near Front for 4th Bde. Men get a house with fire, piano etc. Last night I taught them "Too-ra-loo-ra-loo-ra". As Bing Crosby sang it in "Going My Way", we sang only the chorus.

" The man who has no music in his soul,
Who is not filled with concord of sweet sounds,
Is fit for treasons, stratagems and spoils.
The motions of his soul are dark as night
and his affections dull as Erebus.
Let no such man be trusted."   The Merchant of Venice- Shakespeare

Editor's note
—not quite as Shakespeare wrote it, but close enough under the conditions it was recalled, to leave it as written in the diary.

DEC 9 1944

Some rumored I was sick because there was not so much nonsense in my dispatches from the Front. I plead guilty and promise to make restitution and take my humor seriously as did Will Rogers and John McCormack of blessed memory. General Crerar was too busy to smile much but he did say that Canadians will win this war because they have a better sense of humor than Germans. There are more ways than those of reasoning to find one's way out of depressing circumstances. Keep the pilot light bright.

"Shall we leave gaiety all to the laity?
Cannot the clergy be Irishmen too?" Father O'Flynn- Irish song

DEC 9 1944

Hey Padre tell these new guys about that night in the Aldershot Canteen when you chorded on the piano "My Old Kentucky Home" and noticed two soldiers crying... OK, I'll tell them. The Padre said:"I presume you are Kentuckians", and they said: "No Father, we are musicians!"

...Padre that was a good one about the old Sergeant who came to you to "take the pledge". For you boozers who don't know what that is, it's a pledge or a promise not to 'drink'.
    ...Yeah—drink booze wise guy!
The Padre advised him to pledge not to drink for one week and then come and renew his pledge. What did the old guy say Padre?... Oh yeah, he says: "I'll take it for life or not at all, I always take it for life."

Padre tell us about the guy who couldn't get around the only tree behind your tent and said:
    "I believe I am in the midst of an impenetrable forest."

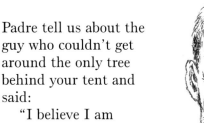

Hey Padre tell them about the guy who bragged about getting seven promotions... He didn't mention seven demotions!

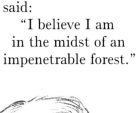

Hey Padre, was he the same one who you said was caught in the corner of the canteen and said: "I believe I am walled in for the night?"

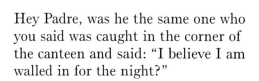

Hey guys the Padre told somebody he was once the president of a debating team— more likely a Liar's Club.

Padre ask these guys your favorite question:
"Who was the father of the seven sons of Zebedee?"

114

DEC 11 1944

I had a talk with "Uncle" Billie Edwards, Bde. carpenter. He is a Protestant and pointed out the climaxes in "Song of Bernadette". The film was shown on the Holland front. He grasped the chief point, being the answer of Bernadette when, from her bed of suffering, she replied to those who suggested a cure by "The Lady". Bernadette said: "The glory of Lourdes is not for me". That should be a lesson for the soldier. His business is to suffer. Someone else reaps the fruit of his suffering but he reaps the eternal recompense, if he goes into battle each day in Peace or War with purity of intention. Nice going Billie.

There was another carpenter who whispered the prayer of Bernadette to Heaven's Queen: "I love You". May she love and guide you till you hang up your weapons of death and be a carpenter full time.

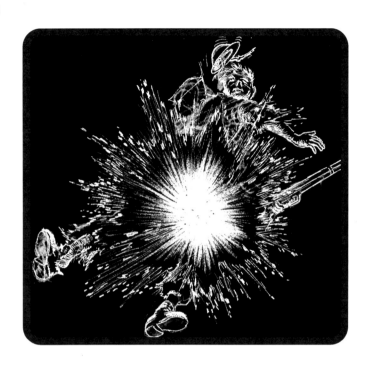

DEC 12 1944

Buried J. Lafferty near Nijmegen. He stepped on a mine. They brought half of him in this morning-two legs, one right and one left—so possibly it was Lafferty— (It has happened otherwise). Lads thought that was a gruesome sight. What doth it matter? He has done his duty to God and Country and will have his resurrection like the rest of us (we hope).

DEC 14 1944

The weirdest sound—a demoralizing effect, then the dull, dead thud of explosion which brings havoc. The concussion almost lifted me from my bed. 'V' rockets can be seen night and day starting their journey. At a meeting of Chaplains someone reminded me that the name Major M.J.Dalton appeared on a little white cross in a temporary cemetery at Fleury-sur-Orne near the big Cave where Civies lived. The Bloke that paints the crosses probably worked in the black-out. I signed the 'Graves Registration Card' at the bottom- names at the top- he read upside down. Therefore, I was dead as a door nail.

DEC 17 1944.

Three Masses-1st in a shelled church a few miles from front, 2nd in beautiful Convent Chapel within shelling range. Nuns singing made us think we were within Angel range. 3rd Mass was in a Billiard Parlor and Pub. Plenty of bombs reaching Antwerp and vicinity. We got out of Cuijk just in time- you can see it burning from here.

I told them today may be their happiest Christmas because the hard things of life bring the best rewards and consolations. (Perhaps I should sneak up Front myself on Christmas. The proof of the pudding is in the eating). If millions eat turkey and live in Corporeal Peace, at least on Christmas, it is because 4th Bde. and countless others are holding the line against perpetrators of evil things. Carry on, oh gallant sons of Canada and some day to your grandchildren yet unborn, you can say: "you were at Mass this blessed Christmas Day and they can eat and live in Peace because Grand-dad held the line one 1944 Christmas for God and Canada". Carry on and hold the Peace.

"Eternal Vigilance is the price of Liberty." Thomas Jefferson My God, what a price.

DEC 1944 – Letter from my Nephew George Dalton Ralph O'Connor

Dear Padre,   Dec 10 1944

    I hope you are still in the best of health and not finding it too cold over there. I suppose the Army is moving too fast for you to settle down and get situated. If it's as cold over there as it is up here I can't imagine how Jerry can stand it, on top of all the inconvenience the allies are giving him.
    It won't be long now before I'm doing some productive flying. It will have been quite a while but it is certainly worth it. I wouldn't give away the experience I've had in the last two years for a million dollars, if I could. I'll be dropping down in France in a Halifax to see you one of these days. I've got a swell bunch of chaps in my crew, all Canadians. I've got only one hope, that my good fortune holds out and we finish a tour and get back to Canada. If we go to the far east we might see Canada sooner. How are the Christmas parcels arriving? I've received several but am afraid I've missed one, possibly burned at Montreal or Halifax. Well, I must be going. Give my regards to Louis and a very Merry Christmas to both of you.

Your devoted nephew,
George

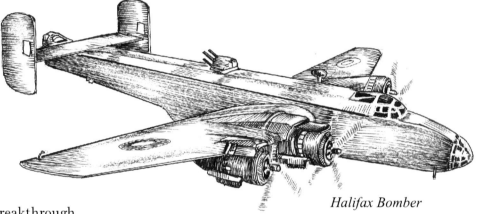

Halifax Bomber

DEC 17 1944

First German counter-attack since D-Day. There is definitely a German breakthrough near Liege. They are now closer to Antwerp than we are. Most men, but not all, are confident they can be held.

The longer I live, the more I am convinced that he who worries in war time, or any other time, is afflicted with a species of atheism. I've pleaded guilty to that in the past. I hope Germans can be held. I'm due in Brussels for retreat after Christmas but roads may be blocked, giving priority to troops that may be rushed up to repel German counter-attack.

DEC 20 1944 Germany visited – Merry Christmas from Germany

Fifth Christmas overseas will be in Mock, a few miles from the German border. I walked a mile or more through a shell torn village, through rich harvest fields still ungarnered due to danger of enemy fire. Catholic pictures abound in all the houses. This is the Catholic part of Germany, near Berganthal, Beek and Nijmegen. No customs or immigration at Border Barrier. Just Canadians on patrol. Houses as in Holland, have low, small beds built in wall of sitting room, but are neat.

This foggy day allowed perusal of our last objective "The Third Reich"; the land that gave us both extremes—Santa Claus and Holy Night and Hitler.

I came. I saw. I returned over a dyke less than 1000 yards from where the enemy lay concealed. This part of Germany has dykes, as in Holland, and more hills than I have seen in six months in Europe. Flooded areas also abound. Barns adjoin houses as in France, Belgium and Holland. At last I saw Germany but no Germans in sight.

DEC 21 1944

First day of winter, little frost, much mud, no snow. Busy week, Confessions etc. Essex Scottish amateur show O.K. A few miles from Front, men are called back from billets due to Parachutists in the area. This is serious business as Americans are being pushed back further south. Show resumed later. Dramatic finale depicted progress through France, Belgium and Holland. As each town unfurled to music of "Land of Hope and Glory", we thought of the brave men who were struck down and buried by the dusty bloody roads awaiting transfer to a Military cemetery.

ESSEX SCOTTISH Battles and possible Battle Honors. So far:

Dieppe, Roquancourt, Elbeuf, Strabraeck, Fleury-sur-Orne, Suicide Hill-152, West end Bains, Falaise, Verrier, Verson, Calouet, Dieppe (second time), Ifs, Potigny, Dunkerque, Etterville, Brettville, Ostend-Belgium, S.Beveland-Holland, Putte, Hoogerheide, Antwerp, Nijmegen.

DEC 22 1944

Christmas boxes pouring in—huge boxes of eats, cigarettes, etc. I look up lads whose ship didn't arrive, (or didn't start) to share the precious gifts and raise their spirits. Thank you all ye soldiers' friends in the new world. God grant you an abundance of temporal and spiritual favors.

Before daylight these men of the 4th Bd, will be at front line again till after New Years. May their Christmas be blessed. Most went to Mass and Communion in a battered church near the front with only feeble candle light due to proximity to Reichwald Forest.

DEC 25 1944   No Peace on Earth yet

Midnight Mass in mostly shelled out Mook Convent Chapel- heard Confessions. German counter attack further south of here spoils their Christmas turkey. Parachutists are dropping here and there.

Early morning and noon—guns barking. Turkey dinner with all the wherewithal. All are bright and happy singing Christmas Carols,(but we knew where our steel hats were). There was a concert after. In keeping with tradition we Officers and Sergeants wait on the men. Sergeants meet in Officers' mess for a wee drop. It is cold, but our last Christmas at war—we think. "Glory to God in the Highest and on Earth, Peace to men of Good Will."

DEC 25 1944

Packing Christmas night for an uncertain move is strong medicine. We know not what our next billets will be, perhaps under roof, perhaps under enemy fire, but not the kind of fire to cheer and warm. It reminds us of another warrior of God. "The Son of God had no place to lay His head." We're warriors even on Christmas day. On the move. We will now be a mobile reserve, ready to strike anywhere fast.

DEC 27 1944   NIJMEGEN HOLLAND

Boy Choristers singing Christmas Carols. I am billeted in a convent with Capt. Grey and Bde. Batman, my best billet in Europe. In eve they sing Christmas and Irish songs taught by the Irish Guards who lived here recently. 9/10 of them can't speak English, but to hear them sing Irish songs with a rich brogue on the Dutch-German border is dramatic. The Protestant boys love the old Dutch Nuns and the young Dutch Nuns and all the people and the clergy.

DEC 29 1944   BOXTEL HOLLAND

Rockets seen daily starting from their base straight up. Saw flying bomb brought down by Ack-Ack. Many bombs going over night and day. On the road again at dusk (for security).It was a long way in the direction of the German break through. Arrived at 1 a.m. after a cold drive and went to bed in the truck.

DEC 31 1944

In the pulpit—"sine lux sine crux, sine aqua benedicta."

"without lights, without a Cross, without Holy Water"

To Sacred Heart Church Boxtel to hear Confessions during Mass and after in the pulpit. Brave soldier lads didn't mind. They are humble. Pastor and seven assistants invite me to the Rectory in evening to discuss future of world events. They have suffered a lot but kept Germans at a distance.

JAN 1 1945   NEW YEAR'S DAY

Mass in stately Chapel at Michaelsgestel. Roads are icy. Many are skating on fields including religious with cassocks. They never take them off even when bicycling. Fields white with snow. We are now on four hours notice to strike in any direction. Germany still has some kick.

JAN 6 1945

Colonel Roy Senior R.C. Canadian Chaplain in Europe had supper with us at 11Fd. Amb.

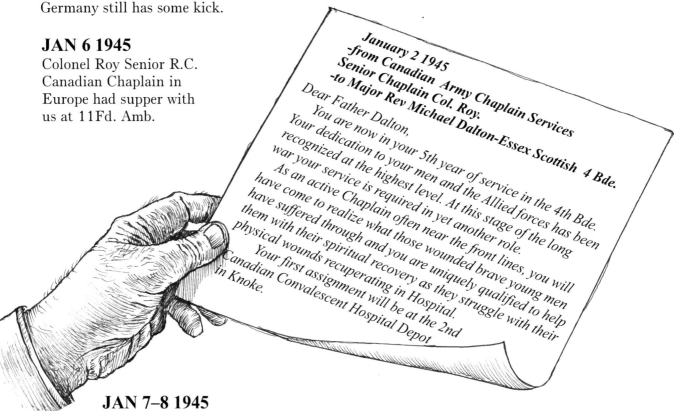

January 2 1945
-from Canadian Army Chaplain Services
Senior Chaplain Col. Roy.
-to Major Rev Michael Dalton-Essex Scottish 4 Bde.

Dear Father Dalton,
You are now in your 5th year of service in the 4th Bde. Your dedication to your men and the Allied forces has been recognized at the highest level. At this stage of the long war your service is required in yet another role.
As an active Chaplain often near the front lines, you will have come to realize what those wounded brave young men have suffered through and you are uniquely qualified to help them with their spiritual recovery as they struggle with their physical wounds recuperating in Hospital.
Your first assignment will be at the 2nd Canadian Convalescent Hospital Depot in Knoke.

JAN 7–8 1945

Back to Nijmegen to same locations. Taught Nuns (school teachers) to sing Irish songs "Too-ra-loo-ra-loo-ra"and "As you Drift along the Shannon". Our guns barking shake windows often to form as it were a kind of accompaniment.
Thousands of kids here have never seen white bread and don't know what Peace is.

JAN 9 1945
Farewell the gallant 4th Bde.
It's time I was going.
It's time I passed on.

A policy has materialized, namely that those on the wrong side of 40, who have borne the heat and burden of the day these long five years, will now be replaced by younger Chaplains. Lads reminded me recently that I had the unique distinction of being in the same 4th Brigade longer than any other Chaplain in this war or the last, and that I was possibly the oldest soldier at the Front including senior officers. It braced me for the inevitable. There were a few Home Runs on the day I left. At my farewell Mass in each Regiment, I preached on the Prodigal Son—result over 200 Communions. A week at Brussels Retreat House is not hard to take. While there Father Victor, a Franciscan, came out after Benediction and was handed a letter. His home and parents were all killed by a flying bomb. He had been in prison and was released by the Allies.

Take it away Father Murphy. You bear the Victory Cross on your hat badge. It is your more spectacular role to actually dethrone the double cross Swastika which is not the Cross of Christ. Let all believers in God unite in daily prayer, that when the blood bath of Europe is over, the Army triumphant will be welcomed in their native land, duty fulfilled, honor unstained, and peace in their hearts. May all those under little white crosses unite with all of us, and with the "Risen Soldier."

JAN 15 1945

Arrived 2nd Canadian Convalescent Hospital Depot Knoke, near Bruges. The Senior Chaplain in Europe wanted someone in this spot who had experience at the Front. It is set up to assist the 2000 fallen heros who linger a few weeks in transit from hospital back to the Front.

Formerly my chief concern was 4th Bde. Now in the wider field, it is the Canadian Army. As the gallant lads bearing the Essex Scottish badge come through, and I meet the daily drafts, it brings me back in memory to the patriotic city of Windsor and its Daily Star and other friends who magnanimously performed the spiritual and corporeal works of mercy, which enabled them to prove on countless Battle Fields that you made a genuine investment for God and Canada.

I need your continued prayers that I may convince our fallen Comrades that Battles are fought and Victories registered in the heart, mind, and soul before they are accomplished in the theatre of Operations. In an effort to grasp what may be going through the mind of a gallant bloke who is off to the wars for the second time, I have volunteered to go back if the young race horses grow prematurely old.

It was my unforgettable privilege to be with them in the uncertain hectic days of the Battle of Britain and in the fierce grim struggles behind the "Great Western Wall". At Dieppe and elsewhere we paused a few days to ask God to strengthen our Army, and pray for dead and next of kin. Unofficially one foggy day, I spent a few fleeting hours in Germany in Kranenburg near Berganthal Holland.

And now when just on the Border of Germany and Victory it is my lot to muse:

"There is a destiny, which shapes our ends,
Rough-hue them as you will."   *Shakespeare, Hamlet: Act 5, Sc 2.*

JAN 15 1945   KNOKE

They say they are roughing it here in 2 Can. Conval. Depot. with central heating, real civilized beds and white table cloths. Airport here guards the Scheldt to Antwerp Port and they get hammered frequently. It's a son of a gun to walk on these icy roads. We walk like ducks but the salt air is good. Canadian winter is good. We have to walk warily—watchful of beach obstacles, mines, barb wire. I get autographs of wounded as these are the Big Shots making History, they are the heroes of a nation of Liberators of a Continent- the Guts of the Army—strong language but it's true. I like to tell it. They like to listen. They forget their wounds for a few fleeting hours.

FEB 2 1945

Every province of Canada represented in new drafts of convalescents. If we walk down main street of any Canadian town after the war we will recognize one of Canada's heroes.

FEB 9 1945

Dance at Grand Hotel. They try as usual to get me to dance. I've got a bad toe.
I'd sooner listen.

FEB 10 1945

Good morning folks. How good it is. General Montgomery starts final offensive- "a dagger pointed at the heart of Germany" said McNaughton of Canada. They reached the Rhine at long last.

FEB 18 1945

Walked eight kilometers to Cappellan, where the Organist plays: "Oh Canada We Stand On Guard For Thee". Is that O.K? Is it a hymn? Can it be played in Church? We dunno. If it wasn't a hymn, haven't Canadians transcribed the music with their noble blood? If Canada freed their corner of Europe for "Liberty and Justice" for the French, Belgians, and Hollanders, and perhaps for Germans and Canada and Mankind, don't we stand on guard for "Thee" with a capital T? We dunno. Cardinal Mercier, the theologian, is dead but organist played it anyway and it helped the fallen heroes to be fallen no longer and heroes in anticipation once more.

> *Breathes there a man*
> *with soul so dead*
> *That never to himself has said*
> *This is my own, my native land*
> *Whose heart within him n'er has yearned*
> *As home his footsteps he has turned*
> *From wandering on a foreign strand".* *Sir Walter Scott*

Is that logical or am I too sentimental? Ask the veteran. There will be one on every Canadian corner if this Holocaust doesn't see the bitter end- exhaustion.

FEB 24 1945

Met Essex Scottish lad wounded in Cleves Germany. Shot by women snipers dressed as men at work. Cleves is compared to Caen in destruction. Civilians hopelessly wandering.

FEB 26 1945

Received letter my sister
Margaret wrote earlier
in February saying:

Dear wrote'r Mike   Lord Thy will be done Feb. 8 1945
George missing

FEB 27 1945

Started a long letter of condolence to my sister Margaret's family—calling it: "Maplehurst Farm Unfinished Symphony". Sent the following short one.

> *Dear O'Connors;*
>
> *Your Feb. 8th letter here.*
>
> *Regret loss of gallant lad. Say Mass tomorrow for him and pray for his return. Wrote to his Chaplain. You should too. "Our cause is just, German bishops have not said as much". (words of Bishop Den O'Connor). George went on his own initiative. Therefore more reward. "For God and Country" is on my M.B.E. medal. Get it from Walter if you wish for George, who was the first of the clan to go down for the count for "God and Country".*
>
> *God may only take 1/10 of your family. Some lose 10/10. Some through planned selfishness have no George to sacrifice. Thank God it is your son and not someone else's who is defending Maplehurst Farm. The first line of defense is not at your Audley Road or Town line. Cardinal Villeneuve said: "War must be won on the battle field, not in Canada".*
>
> *The cream of Maplehurst Harvest has blossomed in splendor. When young George went away to fight against evil things, he reached his Majority. The flower of Maplehurst's gallant manhood shall not blossom in vain. Therefore feed the stock, till the soil, garner the harvests. Keep your chin up. This is your war. Those who by pass the Good Friday of Sacrifice will never get back onto the main route to Easter Sunday.*
>
> *St. John relates: "Now there stood by the Cross Mary His mother". She was just your age Margaret when George was born. Countless unknown mothers stand in spirit with you.*
>
> *God keep them all in the Palm of his Great Hand.*
>
> *M.J.Dalton*

A parcel sent to George in the R.C.A.F. was delivered to me (alternate address), I knew then he was grounded forever. The finding of his "Pay Book" washed ashore at Morayville in Scotland confirmed his death in a Bomber over the North Sea.

Two of my sisters had 22 kids—almost a platoon. My sister Josie had 10 children with three in the service. They all survived. When McKenzie King was stalling in sending zombies O'Seas an officer said to me: "Padre why don't you get married and raise sons for the service"? I replied two of my sisters have four boys in service. How many have you and your sisters? His silence was awful to listen to.

FEB 27 1945

Essex Scottish losses reported heavy on 19th. German tanks break through. Colonel and staff captured and recaptured.

Editor's note Canadian men who were conscripted into the armed forces in 1944 were called Zombies.

MAR 25 1945

Feast of the Annunciation. I remember my Mother's reference to the real thing and visit of St. Elizabeth to Mary. Thoughtless youth doesn't grasp the significance of Theology. It strengthens the faith, but it takes war, long total war on a foreign strand to induce many an old tar to surrender to these divine truths as something just as real as the stuff mowing down our comrades.

MAR 28 1945

Allies running wild beyond the Rhine, cracking over the German Plains. It looks good from here. Mass and Communion daily for all new-comers from the German Theatre. Most of them attend. We meet the new drafts daily, some wounded twice, and the odd one back with his third wound.

MAR 1945

Writing a letter of condolence to my sister Margaret. This is the longest next of kin letter I have ever written. You will find many repetitions. They were intended for this theme is didactic, and repetition is a sound rule of pedagogy. Calling the letter: **" Maplehurst Farm Unfinished Symphony"**.

God accepts a soldier's offering

"Our sincerest laughter, with some pain is fraught,
Our sweetest songs, are those which tell of saddest thought."
To a Skylark, Percy Bysshe Shelley

Excerpts from Unfinished Symphony

The drama of our theme expresses life's struggle, battle and duty done to the bitter end. Here is an assertion of spiritual and patriotic faith in the future despite the stark fact that the lights have gone out in the old world, and God only knows whether they will be lit again in our lifetime.

In the course of his duty George's life's Mass ended, just as he would have wished—with his boots on, on the job, as Captain of his ship. George's father Art's cryptic comment: "Maplehurst is no jail farm" is revealing.

George's mother Margaret said that she wouldn't discourage enlistment for she sensed that George considered it a patriotic duty.

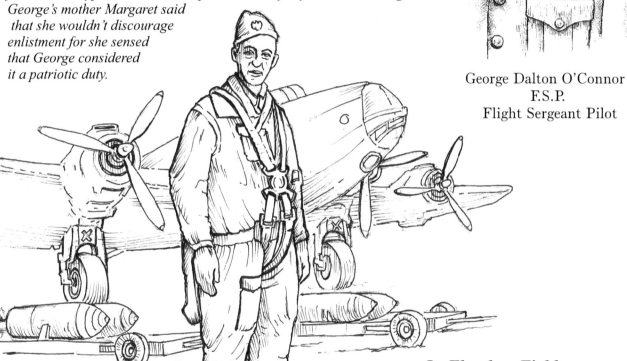

George Dalton O'Connor
F.S.P.
Flight Sergeant Pilot

In Flanders Fields

"In Flanders fields the poppies blow,
Between the crosses, row on row,
That mark our place; and in the sky
The larks, still bravely singing fly,
Scarce heard amid the guns below.

We are the Dead. Short days ago
We lived, felt dawn, saw sunset glow,
Loved and were loved and now we lie
In Flanders fields.

Take up our quarrel with the foe:
To you from failing hands we throw
The torch; be yours to hold it high.
If ye break faith with us who die
We shall not sleep, though poppies grow
In Flanders fields.

Excerpt

*In the last war, in the Ypres sector an M.O. **Dr John McRae** came daily from his dug-out First Aid Station to be greeted by ever lengthening rows of little white crosses. He felt like one coming from the dead and he envisioned his own cross some day, and went back and wrote prophetically as one of the dead. When he was struck down in honored glory the stretcher bearers found some poems in his scattered papers....*

" Maplehurst Farm Unfinished Symphony"

Excerpts continued.

Isn't it just possible that there are some things more devastating than the ugliness of war? Isn't it just possible that future historians many centuries hence, will write about the glorious 20th Century Crusaders liberating nation after nation from the heel of the proud oppressor, for the welfare of God's Kingdom on earth, and for the rights of man, for the preservation of the true faith and its natural concomitants- Justice and Charity, and never breathe a word about:

the blood, the guts, the sweat, the cold, the hunger, the sleepless nights, the trail of little white crosses, the rotting corpses of unburied allied and enemy dead, a field day for rats and maggots, the pathetic sight of unmilked cows searching for food and water and the stinking carcasses of horses, cattle, men, dogs, etc., in every field and back yard, and the legless, eyeless heroes being jeeped back to hospitals.

It happened before. We extol the valor of the Middle Age Crusaders rescuing the Holy Land from the infidels without mentioning the horrors of that War.

The social injustices of the world of our days may long be remembered after the ugliness of the War of our day is forgotten, if the Victories of the latter do not stimulate us to march hand in hand for new victories over the former. We will be looked upon as heartless, a generation of knaves and fools and selfishness, or, a generation with a heart as big as the "Heart of the World" the sacred heart of our Redeemer. We shall nobly save a gasping civilization, so that even the Germans and Japanese and Italians will forever applaud the harmony of our symphony spiritually, politically, and economically and God will forever bless, or we shall cause the slogan of the admiring enemy of the early Christians:

"See how these Christians love one another", Tertullian

to be mutilated and distorted by the enemies of our salvation to: "See how these Christians hate one another".

Monsignor Fulton J. Sheen said: "the only way to drive every enemy from the face of God's earth is to love them". Is it just possible that there are some things more ignoble than war?

Editor's note: These excerpts are only a small part of the complete letter.

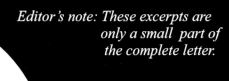

123

Excerpt from a letter from Fr. Mike to his niece
Moira O'Connor – born 1935, George's sister.

Dear Moira;   *1944*

That's a nice way of saying Mary. Your mother Margare knows a lot of tricks like that. Thanks for the box of things you sent to your brother George. I shared it with youngsters of occupied Europe. Margare wrote that if George 'went home', the box would be readdressed to me. He 'went home' with "trailing clouds of glory"- to God from whom he came. If we tune in to the counsel in our coat of arms: "Lord Thy will be done", we will catch up to him someday. These words were the first words your mother wrote to me in reporting:

"George missing."

When you are a little older you will understand what the evils to come may be. If millions of Georges didn't slay the panzered Dragon of irreligion and oppression perhaps some day your parents would be calling for the last sacraments- calling in vain, because the Georges and the Maurices accepted peace at any price. I think their parents would agree with me that their sons and heirs, valiant as they were would then be almost useless.

They found happiness...in time...in their Georges and Maurices. What they want now is happiness that is timeless. It is not what one takes out of life that increases happiness but what one puts into it. If one is continually pouring the milk of human kindness on others some eventually will spill back upon them. Bereaved parents have poured more than a 'milk' of human kindness on the occupied countries, they gave 'cream' of the land- their gallant manhood. They invested their happiness in time- for happiness which is timeless. It pays dividends in this life too. I can tell by the answers to my next-of-kin letters daily pouring in from all over North America and British Isles. They are an education that religion and patriotism are closely allied.

Young lady, You have been an inspiration to me more than once during the conversation that goes on from time to time in the Officers' Mess comprising believers and alleged non-believers. Sometimes they have asked me—whether in good or bad faith, I do not know, why priests don't get married and raise sons as they do for the cause. To hold their attention, I would reply:

"In spite of the fact that I have several hundred spiritual sons who call me "Father" not "Major", my first and foremost reason for remaining a bachelor is out of consideration for the future Mrs. "Father Mike". I learned that one from Father Vincent McNabb C.P. the famous Hyde Park soap box preacher. Hillaire Belloc and I attended his funeral.

Then I would tell of you and my 35 other nephews and nieces, four in the services, and ask if their brothers and sisters had contributed as much, and if they had two sisters with ten kids each and Walter's six making a Platoon, to answer the call of country in future's defense. Always they would give me unanimous dispensation to remain only the Spouse of Christ.

So there you are Moira Macushla. Next time you raise your little supplicant hands in prayer after Communion breath a fervent prayer for —

Uncle Father Mike

O'Connor

Maplehurst
Farm

APR 4 1945

Captain Peatman says I'm due for a 48 hr. leave—first leave in 14 months so it's not hard to take, and Bruges is only 15 miles.

APR 6 1945

Said Mass with Leo XIII Chalice on same Altar Leo said Mass on- Altar of the Holy Blood. I was given kind attention as R.H.L.I. 4th Bde. were the first Canadians to enter Bruges for liberation. The Hun had fled to Leopold Canal and area. A policeman is armed to the teeth during the veneration. Was glad the honor fell to 4th Bde. to save a precious relic (brought from the Holy land in 12th Century) from Nazi tyranny. Church of Notre Dame-Germans stole painting of Michelangelo and his "Madonna in Marble". The empty frame and niche are still there. At 2 o'clock one morning the caretaker, at the point of several guns, had to unlock the caves where they were hidden.

APR 8 1945

Back again to Bruges to witness ordination of 40 priests. There was a sight. There was almost a flood of tears of joy and sorrow, as the parents mingled in the mob to get first blessing. This was done informally right in the Church. The Europeans are like that. We guess our Lord likes them for it.

"Love God and do what you like."
St. Augustine

APR 16 1945

At long last- the first 'real' leave in 15 months—nine days. I saw Paris during a week's course at the beautiful University of Paris. The Sorbonne is now controlled by non-Catholic teachers but Theologians discuss "Real Presence" —a main painting on the wall. I visited Breendock, and talked to men still in the striped uniforms of the political prisoners, I visited all places of world fame— the Sorbonne where Thomas Aquinas taught, the Arc de Triomphe, Tomb of Napoleon, Place de Concorde, Church of Sacred Heart, Notre Dame. Boy what a town, but I must go on to Lisieux.

The Padre and some new friends at the University of Paris.

APR 21 1945

Lisieux and St. Theresa "Little Flower" are synonymous to the World. Desolation in town—3000 killed in D-Day air raids, most still smelling in gigantic ruins. Ah—a breath of sanctity in Carmelite Church. Mass for "me" beside the body of St. Theresa. Afternoon—to her original tomb and that of Mr. Martin, her father, in parish cemetery. I also saw shrapnelled graves opened. Poem by Fr. C. Coughlin my Assumption teacher:

MAY 4 1945

V. Day for Canadians. Deo Gratias.

"Oh scatter roses through this hour
Dear Theresa, our little flower."

MAY 5 1945

Just another Saturday.

MAY 6 1945

Belgium White Brigade wreck houses of collaborators with Germans- senseless waste of property. We went to war to fight against such mob violence. Let Justice try them. Mob vindictive punishment is dangerous. Furniture broken and thrown on streets. Waste of food and clothes in stores and thousands seem to applaud. Police are helpless. So are we. They rule themselves (or misrule). Returned prisoners from German suffering in camps may have started it. I understand this is general throughout Belgium. If I were Eisenhower I would cut off their rations till they stopped the nonsense. Peace rumors increasing. It is too good to be true.

MAY 7 1945

The day we have long awaited.
J.L. Swift Ltd. Toronto Ontario, just entered my billet with the good news. A lot of rambling thoughts come and go as we look out the window and see Europe at peace. Germany signed unconditional surrender on May fourth.

WAR ENDS IN EUROPE
EXTRA Special edition EXTRA
Canadians rejoice

The Prime Minister said that...

EUROPE WAR ENDS
EXTRA UNCONDITIONAL SURRENDER
NAZIS QUIT
In Remaining Pockets

Reims, France—(AP)–Germany surrendered unconditionally to the Western Allies and Russia at 2:41 A.M. French time today (8:41 P.M. EWT Sunday). The surrender took place at a little red sch...
...headquraters of Gen. Eisenhower. The su...

News Chronicle
4 a.M. Edition

VICTORY ISSUE May 8. 1945

VICTORY ISSUE May 8 1945

TODAY IS V DAY
Today and tomorrow are national holidays: Churchill speaks at 3 p.m., the King at 9

Today is V Day and a public Holiday , tomorrow is V Day plus one and is also a Holiday This was announced last night

In Piccadilly the hub of all celebration thousands upon thousands of people, airmen infantry men, sailors of all the Allies, girls in blue and girls in khaki milled around the circus with civilians.

MAY 7 1945

A Belgium lady invited me to breakfast after Mass to celebrate the victory with a special treat. She called it cheval—I called it horsemeat—4 dollars a pound. They forgot to take the harness off. I couldn't tell her that in French, so I ate it.

Editor's note May 5th was the Padre's birthday,
the same day as his brother Dennis.

May 22 1945

I left my office at 10 o'clock p.m. Major Campbell, Chrysler dealer from Vancouver met me at the door. "Major Fred Tilston won the V.C." (Victoria Cross). Fred went to St. Alphonsus Church Windsor and was Essex Scottish Adjutant since Dieppe.

Scores of times he arranged time and place of Mass for me and attended himself in England and between battles. It wasn't desperate battle that influenced him to give reasonable service to his Creator; rather it was his reasonable service which strengthened him to do desperate battle for God and Country. If Freddy was listening now I think he'd say "Amen". It's a V.C. for Essex Scottish, for St. Alphonsus Parish; a V.C. For Canadian Army, for all lovers of justice, truth and freedom.

Where does poor Fred come in? What does he get out of it? Nothing but ephemeral praise and honor.

"They shot off his legs, So he lay down his arms." He put his two big feet in it because he wasn't interested in "defeat." He left them in it. He shall never walk on those feet again below the knees.

"Sic transit gloria mundi." (Thus passes, the glory of the world- Worldly things are fleeting.)

"The tall lean frame was racked with pain. One leg hung in shreds, the other was shattered. But the face burned beyond recognition by powder blast still grinned. The lips moved: "tell Doc, we held."
That was Fred Tilston V.C."

Quoted in the diary from Sgt. Joe Greaves (Staff writer Maple Leaf)

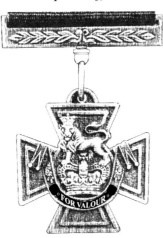

The Victoria Cross is a Military Decoration awarded for Valour, "In the Face of the Enemy"

Major Frederick A. Tilston V. C.

MAY 26 1945

65 Subdeacons ordained in Bruges Cathedral. Mothers and friends rush up to greet them just outside the huge sanctuary. There was a sight— a different sort of tear than what we usually see in war-torn towns.

JUN 10 1945
At Sacred Heart Church, Knoke, I announced the death of their pastor in Belson Concentration Camp. He assisted R.A.F. who bailed out, to get back to England. Several dozen priests died there. Another martyr for Christianity.

JUN 14 1945
To Benedictine Abbey near Bruges, a seven kilo bike ride with Fr. Joe Ghekiere. Germans unknowingly guarded Belgium colors and flags of several dozen Regiments. They were hidden between partitions the day before Belgium collapsed in 1940.

JUN 16 1945
Three old sweats on wrong side of 40; Fathers Kelly from P.E.I., O'Leary from Sudbury and myself, yanked out of Europe to give experience to three younger race horses rusting in England.

JUN 17–19 1945
Hailed a jeep going to Nijmegen, dinner in Antwerp, on to Mook, Reichwald, Cleves, which was almost flat. Henry VIII got Anne there. Wagner got inspiration. On to Hochwald, where Major Fred Tilson, Essex Scottish won V.C. To Cologne, crossed the Rhine on President Roosevelt Bridge near Xanten. Down to great Rubin District with hundreds of empty smoke stacks and thousands in ruins. Dusseldorf is a bad mess.

To Cologne, its majestic Cathedral still standing in the ruins of ½ million people's destroyed city. Its windows are gone but shrapnelled walls are repairable.
Many people are living in the ruins. Some speak good English and seem friendly, but watch 'em. To Liege Belgium for the night. Next morning the train to Brussels over hilly country similar to England, but not so wooded.

JUN 21 1945

Brussels Air Port. Met Col. McCorkell, Brigadier Campbell and a few
others. I got excess baggage on, suggesting that the scales could be wrong.
We traveled in a Dakota twin-engine mail plane sitting on pieces of mail.

Just a year ago there were V-1 flying bombs and shelling over the white cliffs of
Dover. Our invasion of Europe was a slower process. Jerry had planes fly over the
night we landed. We had to stay in Liberty ships all night among thousands of
crafts. Some were sunk. Battle field of air over the Kent hop fields is still there,
unscathed by devastations of war. There are no poppies or wings in the sky, no
crosses to mark their place, but many brave lads made the supreme sacrifice in
no man's land of sky and air, to give us a breathing spell to mobilize the might
to bring the Hun to his knees, physically and figuratively.

"There'll be Blue Birds over The White Cliffs of Dover"
a very popular WW 2 song sung by Vera Lynn. Lyrics by Nat Burton and Walter Kent.

Biggin Hill Air Port, Kent, about 25 miles south of London came into sight.
We often thought of Paddy Finuecane, the intrepid Irish Wing Commander, who
struck down umpteen enemy planes. One day over the French coast he radioed,
"This is it fellows" as he received a direct hit. Due to his prowess and Churchill's
historic, *"few to whom never in the field of human conflicts was so much owed by so many."*
that we are able to say in peace and security "This is it, fellows", on hovering
over Biggin Hill Air Field. It might have been different. It almost was. We
might have been in bondage. God save the R.A.F. who did the spade work in
the sky to enable us to plod along to V.E. Day. To London by bus. Flying bomb
and rocket damage plenty in parts. To Aldershot by train, then to Leipsig Barracks
dedicated by Kaiser Will before the last war. Aldershot hasn't changed much. I
rambled around Maida Barracks, home of 1940 Essex Scottish, and met all strange
faces. Thousands milling around the great military city anxious to get home.

JUN 28 1945

Packed legless Major Fred Tilston V.C. into a car to Greyshot Camp to meet dozens of returned Dieppe prisoners. Quite a job remembering names since August 1942 but faces haven't changed much after three years of prison fare. They are still young. First man I met was Mickey McManus, and then Fred Kawalski, the three Percy brothers, Robertson, Lloyd Lauzon, choir soloist, Colleen Scarf, that lad with the million dollar smile, Pilon, Shepperd, Windover, Sterling, one of the Wilson Park hockey players opposite O.L.P.S. and dozens of others. Dinner at Royal Anchor Hotel Liphook where Nelson, the great sailor, used to dine on route to his fleet at Portsmouth. Our car was parked under the spreading Chestnut tree made famous by Longfellow.

"Under the spreading Chestnut tree
The village smithy stands;"   Henry Wadsworth
Longfellow

Tennyson's home Hazelmere still magnificent. We brought Freddie home in good spirits.

JUL 2 1945

Celebration of Dominions Day had filled most of Westminster Cathedral. The King and Queen and Princess Elizabeth stepped into Westminster Abbey as we passed. The princess hasn't heard of V.E. Day. She still wore an A.T.S. uniform.

JUL 4 1945

Canadians got dates mixed up so celebrated. I thought noise was election crowds after Churchill's defeat. Hundreds impatient to get home, prowl Aldershot streets breaking windows. Provosts and police powerless in mob. There are many thousands here.

JUL 5 1945

Same thing only more so. Plate glass all over the streets this morning as I walked downtown to buy a few things. Citizens are annoyed but most of them are still civil and courteous. Canadians condemned such misrule in Belgium when the prisoners came home to break up collaborators' homes—"Judge not and ye shall not be judged". Several hundred C.W.A.C.'s now in town with a good hand. The fairer sex may mitigate the damage to Canada's prestige by the thoughtless heroes. Breaking huge plate glass windows won't bring more shops- or will it? 100 arrested and may be court-martialled.

JUL 7 1945

Arrived at 3 Canadian Repat Depot at Cove near Farnborough. Thousands pass through this camp of wooden huts out in the country on their way to Burma and home. These huts look like rows of sheep barns but inside they are comfortable, but drab. When we think of trench life a year ago these camps take on aspects of luxury hotels.

JUL 14 1945

Several thousand in camp now. I talked to them on parade square over a loud speaker. Two camps have small Chapels thanks to the zeal of my predecessors. Batman Louis is a handyman, carpenter, typist and lo and behold sits down at a portable altar and plays and sings. The lusty voices of men who have fought and won join in. Chapel Huts look like barns but within are gems. In memory of my parents I dedicate them, "St. John's Cathedral and St. Mary's Basilica".

AUG 7–19 1945

Retreat with 80 British priests. Many lost homes, schools and churches. Some buried forever beneath the ruins missed the retreat.

AUG 15–16   V. J. Day Victory in Japan

Masses, prayers of thanksgiving, shows, dances. The lads didn't break any windows but they had an uncorking good time. Leave anticipated at Newman Centenary at Beaumont College Windsor. There will be a:

"Flow of Soul and a Feast of Reason." Alexander Pope- Imitations of Horace

NOV 6 1945

What- no entries since August. I'm not mentioning names but someone must be loafing.100 acres of huts to attend to comes first. That Newman leave was better than it was cracked up to be—made a new man of an exhausted Veteran.

THURSDAY NOV 8 1945   A MEMORABLE DAY

Just said "Good Bye and God speed" to the veterans of dear old Essex Scottish of six years of blessed memory. And so, "Goodnight" to this page of history stretching from War to Peace—Invasion—to Retreat—Amen.

I would like to be going with them, but am asked to stay- a hard decision but an easy alternative. Chaplains are encouraged to "give their last full measure of devotion" for God and Country. I am now in a Retreat House engaged in the "Battle for Peace" where 4000 gallant blokes left off in actual combat in defense of God-given inalienable rights of Christian citizenship. It is fitting—*"dignum et justum est" (dignified and just)* that someone should remain to help mould a spiritual monument to their memory—to strengthen spiritual lives of low point Essex Scottish and countless others who may pass through this school as 800 Canadians had already.

This is not first time I said "Good bye and God Bless you" to the gallant outfit on eve of departure to another land. I said the same to countless thousands as they trudged courageously into "no man's land" that all lovers of freedom and democracy may enjoy the privilege of going back to a safer land—the land of the "Maple leaf".The responsibility of Warriors was great. They accepted it with a prayer on their lips. Our responsibility is as great and as serious. Sweat is cheaper than blood. (You can say that again). Let us go back to help build a cleaner world for their widows, orphans, parents and friends to be worthy of their blood, in justice to ourselves- and to safeguard the heritage of children yet unborn. That is all Canada asks. We can do no more. We dare not do less—So help us God.

NOV 8 1945

At Camp adjutant's office, Aldershot, getting landing card and ticket to Dublin.
A terrific explosion 15 yards away. A ball of fire and a pall of smoke from a jet
plane crashed between two huts. All on fire—I rushed to a phone and called central.
Pilot and Canadian on street killed. Many missed death by a hair's breadth.
Our jeep had just left the spot. Group Captain Wilson, who set world record of
666 mph. appeared. Famous Farnboro experimental station just a mile away.

NOV 11 1945.

Armistice Day. Requiem High Mass for George O'Connor. All Canadian Choir. Room
at Canadian Legion—few steps from Westminster Cathedral—then on to Ireland. First
time to wear a black suit in 2½ years. We can't go into Eire in uniform. It's not as warm
as battle dress in November winds, but warmth of Erin's hearts will balance that out.

And so ends the first Armistice day in Peace since 1938.

FEB 12 1946.

Reveille 5 a.m. London to Rome non-stop. Left Croydon Air Port- 8:30 a.m.,
an hour late. Port badly battered in 1940. Fly in American Dakota, an old crate
from which parachutists leaped into battle and wounded were brought back in
stretchers. Lots of mail and 14 passengers for Athens. Breviary, morning prayer
and meditation way up in the clouds. Average 180 mph. Trip five hrs. France
in sight- a more peaceful approach than our D-Day 1944. Over Le Havre- 900
miles to Rome. It takes a week by sea. Air pockets over the Alps—snow white
and rugged—make rough riding for writing in this diary, plus cold hands.
There is no heat in this sky buggy; loose fitting doors, drafty and cold. All
are dressed up in overcoats and gloves (except when scribbling this). Nice in sight
at foot of snow-clad Alps—nice city. Corsica sighted on far right. Napoleon
was born there. Sea and water, water everywhere and not a drop to drink.

Rome looks splendid. St. Peter's Dome looks small from the top. Safe landing at
Italian airport battered by war. Weather like an April day, on to the Continental
Hotel. Good night Rome of Ancient splendor and modern Spiritual romance.
Three days in Rome, then south in a lorry past many battlefields to British and
Canadian Cemetery at foot of Mt. Cassino with 4000 white crosses and Indian
Tombstones. Americans made good bad job of 3rd century Abbey and ancient town.

FEB 13–14 1946

Morn—called Vatican to find hours of Papal Audience. Pope has a cold; audience canceled. Lots of fruit in the stores. Some people look well fed and are well dressed. Prices super high for all things. Mass on Blessed Virgin's Altar in St. Mary Majors Basilica. During Mass I thought of Italian priest who said his first Mass at same altar. His name—Pius XII. To the Opera in evening.

FEB 16–19 1946

I saw St. Paul's Colosseum, Roman Baths, Triumphal Arch of Constantine, Catacombs of St. Sebastian where Sts. Peter and Paul were originally buried. Mass at altar of St. Maritiani. Gave Communion to four Italians—former enemies. First Mass offered for my Mother and Dad. To Dome of St. Peter's to view Vatican City. I had a Tour of Vatican- 2½ miles of museum, paintings, sculptures, tapestries, Sistine Chapel etc.

With others, I meet the Pope. He enters with a long stride and speaks to each one separately who kiss his ring. He gave each a medal and a "God Bless You." When I told him where I was from he repeated with keen interest: "Windsor- God Bless You."

"Thy blessing like a ray of light
Is on the water day and night
And like a beacon guides me home." From Memoriam, Tennyson

FEB 20–21 1946

The Pope again—enters in his gustatorial chair supported by 12 men in fancy uniforms entering the long hall, blessing all on each side with "awful" sincerity. He looks old and worn. People all cheer "Viva le Papa".

Third sight of the Holy Father—my ticket puts me opposite his throne, about 100 feet away, a good view as each Cardinal ascends for the Red Hat. Music is classic and modern by Sistine Choir. Brilliant lighting—scores of photographers and movie cameras. Princes of Church and State, High-Ranking Soldiers, Knights of Malta—everybody. The Vicar of Christ upon the earth sang the Blessing in a high resonant tenor voice. Later the Pope sits motionless with mitre. A vision of the Pope, worn by years of war as he is borne out on the chair, is a vision of a blessing from the highest moral authority in the world.

"Benedictat vos omnipotens Deus, Pater et Filius et Spiritus Sanctus."

May almighty God bless you, the Father and the Son and the Holy Spirit

I saw Rome...I saw the Pope

FEB 23–24 1946

Many poor people, old and young, are begging in streets. Going back to hotel I tripped over a woman and her child in the dim-lighted street asleep on the pavement with their alms cup only partially filled. To church near airport. Only people in church are women in rags. To Marseilles, the biggest airport I have ever seen. 4½ hrs to Croydon.

"God must have loved the poor, he made so many of them." (Lincoln I think.)

FEB 25 1946

Tried to call my sister Toni in American Army—no luck. Evening to Aldershot, living a few blocks from wrecked British Military Prison where 400 convicts mutinied. From Red Cross got message from Toni- she would try to come to London. Snow is falling.

MAR 1 1946

To 1 Repat "at long last"- not as an observer this time, but for the real thing- Repatriation to Canada. No ship available for a few days so back into London. No word from Toni yet.

MAR 2 1946

On way to Sunday Mass when Sister Toni calls. To Albert Hall to hear "Beethoven's Mass in D", with an exquisite choir. Malcolm Sargent directs choir and orchestra.

MAR 4 1946

Caesar and Cleopatra and Toni and Mike all meet at Marble Arch Odeon Theatre. We let the former do the acting—walked to Hyde Park to hear outdoor audience. Eve to Compline at Westminster Cathedral. First time I have seen snow in March in my 6th English winter.

MAR 1946

Lunch at A.R.C. Madame Tussaud's Wax Works. Toni to tour London, I to Repat Depot to get ready for Boat.

MAR 6 1946

To Southampton to embark on "Isle de France". 8000 vets crowded into a ship
built for 2000. Billeted in upper bunk. Major Cam Ritchie in same. Mass
candles put near roof for early Mass were twisted by heat from pipes—same here.

MAR 7 1946

Mass everyday in Chapel. Nurses, soldiers etc. attend. When sea is rough I stagger at
the altar. There is always a danger of spilling wine. Only two meals a day, three shifts
for each meal—so no time for noon meal. Salt water baths. If you forgot to fill a water
bottle in morning, you drank salt water or bought it from other blokes. If you want to
walk, the only chance is to get up before dawn, before 8000 vets pack the corridors. I did.

We were not afraid of submarines, as on the way over. We were also not afraid we were
going to a lost cause. I never was. I didn't know enough. England was defeated at the
"Fall of France" and didn't know it, so carried on. I was the first to tell Col. Pearson
at Camp Borden in Canada that France had fallen. I had heard it on the radio.

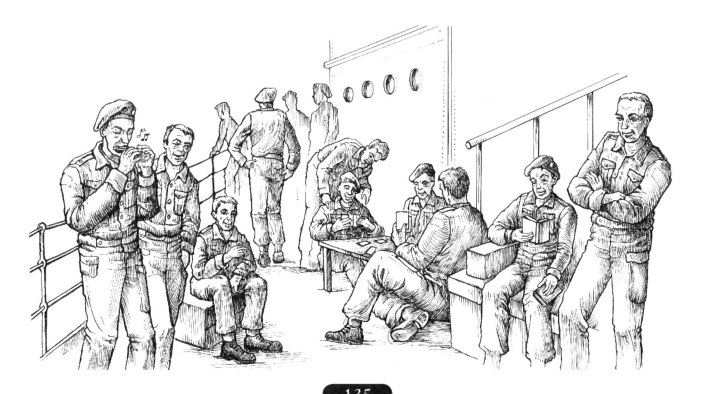

MAR 17 1946 St. Pat's Day

Landed at Halifax Nova Scotia. I would have kissed the ground of Canada if people were not looking. While waiting for the train I walked to Cathedral High Mass in a beautiful church, with beautiful vestments. I had one for six years, black on one side and white on the other. I used the black side too often. I was like a kid looking at Christmas toys. I gawked into grocery store windows, looking at oranges, bananas, fresh fruit etc. In England stores have potatoes, turnips, onions, etc. (a poor show).

Arrival in Toronto

On the train I saw my sister Margare's farm from the 'back 50'. I saw Art-Margare's husband, walking around the farm truck. (That evening I checked the time. It was he). At the Canadian National Exposition Grounds the trains unloaded. Margare had almost emptied the Colleges and Schools of Toronto to meet me. I was lost and couldn't find them. Then I found my sister and her kids. (They found me).

I couldn't talk. Honest to God. I'll tell you why. Blood is thicker than water. One of Margaret's ten kids was missing, missing forever. If he and countless others were not missing, I would be missing too, in slavery in a foreign strand.

George Dalton O'Connor was buried with his four-engine bomber, where the North Sea sang his Requiem.

*Entering Halifax Harbor
March 1946*

Margaret was braver than I. After six months missing, the government reported George "presumed dead". His mother played and sang his Requiem Mass. She was the parish organist. Spartan Mothers in Greece told their sons, as they went to war: "Come home with your shields or upon them."

LATER: At Goderich, I was called to officiate at a church. There was a solemn ceremony for 1000 College boys who will never return. Some I had buried.

SOME MONTHS LATER.
For the last time I saluted the
King's Commission leaving
H.Q. in London Ontario
after demobilization.
On saluting the guards at
the gate, I was lonesome.

ERECTED
GOVERNMENT
CANADA

WOLSELEY BARRACKS
INFANTRY SCHOOL
BUILDING

THIS BUILDING, TYPICAL OF MILITARY
ARCHITECTURE OF ITS PERIOD, WAS
BUILT IN 1886 TO PROVIDE QUARTERS
FOR THE RECENTLY AUTHORIZED "D"
COMPANY, INFANTRY SCHOOL CORPS, AN
EARLY STEP IN THE DEVELOPMENT OF
THE PERMANENT FORCES OF CANADA. IN
1901, AFTER THREE CHANGES, THE CORPS
WAS RENAMED THE ROYAL CANADIAN
REGIMENT. REGIMENTAL HEADQUARTERS
MOVED HERE IN 1923.

DURING THE YEARS 1914-18 AND
1939-45 WHILE THE REGIMENT WAS
ON ACTIVE SERVICE THE BUILDING
WAS USED FOR RECRUITING, TRAINING
AND DEMOBILIZATION. THE REGIMENT
RETURNED TO THE BARRACKS IN 1953.

HISTORIC SITES AND MONUMENTS
BOARD OF CANADA

After ordination in 1932, Fr. Mike became assistant pastor in the city of Windsor at Holy Name Church and St. Alphonsus Church. After the war he worked tirelessly as the pastor in Windsor at Most Precious Blood, in Woodslee at St John's Parish, and in Kingsville, at St. John de Brebeuf Church.
As an advocate of ecumenism, and a long distance walker he visited all homes in the communities where he lived, both Catholic and Protestant.

He was invited to speak at many schools and universities and in 1957 was presented with the Order of Alhambra. He was welcomed at all local Legions and in the Canada's Centennial year 1967, the Royal Canadian Legion named him: "Veteran of the Year".
He was also named "Citizen of the Week". At age 98 he was given the AIR CANADA "Heart of Gold" award for his outstanding contributions to his community. Several of the Padre's diary written entries were included with diary photographs in a 2003 film production for History Televison. The film was called "From a Place called War".

In 2005 the city of London, Ontario honored him by naming an avenue "Father Dalton Avenue". During his senior years his nephew Cletus Dalton became his frequent driver and helpful companion. He spent his last years entertaining at family reunions and living actively as pastor in Crescent Care Home for Seniors in Courtland Ontario until 2009. Then, as he would have put it, he "received his final reward" in his 107th year.

Rev. Michael J. Dalton

The Padre's tombstone is in his home community of Kingsbridge, in St. Joseph's Church cemetery. The tombstone is shown depicting both sides- one bearing the names of Michael's parents Mary and Morgan.

The Padre arrived in Scotland in June 1940. In July 1944, after four years in England, he went to France, Belgium, and Holland to the border of Germany. In January 1945 he was sent back to Belgium and in June 1945 to England. After a side trip to Rome, he returned to Canada in March 1946. His sister Margaret's family met him at the train station and returned to their home in Pickering. Later when he was driving, Fr. Mike turned onto the wrong side of the road and an alarmed Margaret quickly realized that her brother would need time to get used to driving on the right side. Some time later, after the Padre returned to Windsor and visited family in Kingsbridge. Margaret arranged for her son, 17 year old Denis O'Connor, to drive the Padre 420 miles to visit a relative in Timmins for a holiday. Returning to Windsor he was made Pastor of a large new parish called Most Precious Blood.

The following are just some of the places traveled to or through that the Padre mentions in his diary.

IN THE UNITED KINGDOM:
1-Gourock
2-Aldershot
3-Grosvenor house (London)
4- leaves to Eire (Ireland).
5-Isle of Wight
6-Inverness
7-Windermere
8-Brookwood Cemetery
9-Birmingham
10-Isle of Man
11-Horsham
12-Scilly Isle
13-Canterbury
14-Dover
15-Bognor Regis
16-New Haven

IN EUROPE:
17-La Valette
18-Verson
19- IFS
20-Verrieres
21-Caen
22-Louvigny
23-Roguancourt
24-Falaise
25-Rouen
26-Dieppe
27-Saint Omer
28-Ypres
29-Antwerp
30-Brussels
31-Putte
32-Hoogeride
33-Nijmegen
34-Kranenburg
35-Grosebeek
36-Knoke

-Halifax to Gourock Scotland- July 30 1940

Southampton to Halifax- March 6 1946

Padre's trip to Rome Feb. 12-23 1946

After the Padre returned to Knoke the Regiment continued into Germany to Hochwald-**37**, Xanten-**38**, Assen-**39,** Groningen-**40**, Oldenburg-**41**, and North West Germany -**42**.
On V.E. Day May 8,1945 the Essex Scottish Regiment moved to its first policing duty at Huntlosen- **43**, south of Oldenburg. On July 8 operational duties for the Essex Scottish ceased.

ESSEX SCOTTISH HONOUR ROLL

OFFICERS

Capt. J. T. Anderson
Lieut. A. K. Blois
Capt. L. C. Bond
Lieut. R. H. Burns
Lieut. T. E. Campbell.
Lieut. J. A. Chandler
Lieut. G. E. Chester
Lieut. J. O. Combe
Capt. G. O. Cowling
Capt. H. E. Dann
Capt. C. T. Elliot
Lieut. W. J. R. Fogerty
Lieut. W. R. Graham
Capt. P. M. Grandjean
Lieut. A. D. Green
Major T. E. Hayhurst
Lieut. K. G. Jeanneret
Lieut. G. H. Jones

Lieut. S. W. Jones
Lieut. P. E. E. Lamontagne
Lieut. P. O. Lee
Lieut. H. E. Lindal
Lieut. T. E. Martin
Lieut. W. L. Moore
Lieut. R. S. Morgan
Lieut. D. A. Muir
Lieut. F. E. Mullins
Lieut. A. Murrison
Lieut. J. C. Palms
Lieut. I. A. C. Phillips
Lieut. G. A. Ponsford
Lieut. J. Stewart, D.C.M.
Lieut. W. H. Vester
Capt. J. S. Watt
Lieut. J. D. Williams
Major J. A. Willis

OTHER RANKS

Pte. S. F. T. Acheson
Pte. C. P. Adams
Pte. H. Albertson
Pte. B. M. Alexander
Pte. G. Alexander
Pte. T. W. Alexander
Pte. E. W. Allen
Pte. C. Alles
Pte. C. R. Anderson
Pte. I. H. Anderson
Pte. L. Andrew
Pte. W. Andrijouski
Pte. R. N. Armstrong
Pte. A. Arsenault
Sergt. A. E. Arthur
Pte. W. K. Ash
Pte. J. E. Aurand
Pte. L. G. Avey
Pte. W. H. Balch
Pte. J. Ballmer
Pte. J. L. Balog
Pte. A. H. Balson
Cpl. K. R. Bannister
Pte. W. E. Banyard
Pte. N. A. Barnard
Pte. G. W. Barnet
Pte. G. E. Barrett
Pte. E. C. Bartholomew
Pte. A. Baylis
Pte. R. Belcourt
Pte. A. E. Bell
Pte. C. E. Bennett
Pte. S. Berger
Pte. E. Bessey
Pte. J. F. Beston
Pte. G. Bezenar
Cpl. G. T. Birch
Cpl. T. S. Bissett
Pte. F. Bizovy
Pte. W. Black
Cpl. J. P. Boland
Pte. K. W. Bolitho
Pte. G. R. Borthwick
Pte. D. J. Bourque

Pte. C. O. Bowers
Pte. W. A. Boyd
Pte. H. G. Boyden
Cpl. G. Bradshaw
Pte. O. C. Brandon
Cpl. M. A. Brash
Pte. G. T. Brewer
Pte. C. J. R. Briscoe
Cpl. R. M. Bristol
Pte. E. F. Brox
Cpl. L. D. Brule
L./Sgt. R. E. A. Burdick
Pte. C. S. Burk
Pte. M. T. Burke
Pte. C. F. Burling
Sergt. W. W. Buszowski
Pte. R. Butler
L./Sgt. A. Cadman
Pte. H. R. Calberg
Pte. C. H. Campbell
Pte. B. H. R. Capnerhurst
Pte. C. A. Carey
Pte. E. J. Carleton
Pte. F. Carriere
Cpl. H. Carson
Pte. D. R. Carter
Pte. J. H. Cerullo
Pte. A. T. Chadwick
Cpl. R. E. Chamberlain
Pte. H. D. Chamberlain
Pte. A. L. Chambers
L./Sgt. A. R. Charette
L./Cpl. J. D. Charlebois
Pte. H. Cherry
Pte. V. J. Chevalier
Pte. J. P. Chomyn
Sergt. E. G. Ciphery
Pte. G. G. Clark
Pte. L. F. Clark
Cpl. I. Clarke
Pte. J. L. Clarke
Pte. R. A. Cline
Pte. M. Cloutier
Pte. K. G. Cochrane

OTHER RANKS

Cpl. T. J. Cochrane
Pte. C. K. Collison
Pte. D. E. Comeau
Pte. D. P. Conway
L./Cpl. J. W. Cook
Pte. W. Cook
Pte. J. Cooke
Pte. D. Corbiere
Pte. A. R. Cormier
L./Cpl. L. J. Cormier
Cpl. R. Cousineau
Pte. W. L. Cousineau
Pte. D. E. Couture
Pte. E. Couvia
L./Cpl. W. R. Cox
L./Cpl. R. J. Crooke
Pte. A. M. Cudmore
Pte. H. E. Cullimore
Pte. W. R. Cunningham
Pte. J. A. Curoe
Cpl. G. I. Currie
Pte. I. P. M. Currie
Pte. R. C. Curtis
Pte. R. D. Davidson
Pte. W. J. Dawes
Pte. F. A. Dawson
Pte. G. A. Dean
Pte. F. J. Delisle
Pte. L. Delorme
Pte. W. I. Dennis
Pte. G. C. Deschaine
Pte. J. J. F. Desjardins
Pte. R. Devos
Pte. R. B. Dewolfe
Pte. A. G. Dixon
Pte. G. A. Dixon
C.Q.M.S. C. Donald
L./Cpl. E. R. Donnelly
Pte. C. Dorey
Pte. R. C. Downey
L./Cpl. A. C. W. Driscoll
Pte. S. Drummond
Pte. W. D. Duckworth
Pte. A. Duncan
Pte. W. G. Duncan
Pte. D. W. Dunnett
Cpl. W. G. Durey
Pte. C. Durocher
Pte. C. P. East
Pte. G. F. Eastes
Pte. J. R. Ednie
L./Cpl. E. L. Eisenmenger
Pte. N. G. Ellis
Pte. R. D. Ellis
Pte. V. G. Errey
Cpl. L. Evans
Pte. H. J. Falsetto
L./Cpl. M. W. Farrell
Pte. G. R. Faubert
Pte. R. W. Faubert
Cpl. F. Ferrari
Pte. G. H. Ferrari
Pte. O. W. Fischer
Pte. W. L. Fish
Cpl. E. N. Fleming
Pte. W. L. Floyd

Pte. W. G. Foley
Pte. K. J. Ford
Pte. A. F. Forsbrey
L./Cpl. J. A. Foster
Pte. W. F. Fowler
Cpl. A. Fox
Pte. H. H. Fox
Pte. J. W. Fradgley
L./Cpl. D. E. Franklin
L./Cpl. K. L. Fried
Pte. R. J. Fritzell
Cpl. A. C. Gall
Pte. H. W. Gallant
Pte. F. C. Gatacre
Cpl. J. A. Gatschene
Pte. E. J. Gault
Pte. F. W. Gehl
Pte. S. George
Pte. E. H. Gerrie
Pte. W. H. Giffen
Pte. C. W. Gilchrist
Pte. H. M. Gilkinson
Pte. J. P. Gill
Pte. D. R. Gleave
L./Cpl. H. L. Godfrey
Pte. J. A. G. Godfrey
Pte. J. Gorda
Pte. R. M. Gordon
Pte. J. Goulet
Pte. J. Gross
Cpl. L. J. Guay
Pte. L. W. Gulliver
Pte. R. T. Haines
Pte. M. Haluik
Pte. D. M. Hancock
Cpl. L. L. Hanley
Pte. P. C. Hanson
Pte. G. H. Harmon
Pte. E. E. Hartling
Pte. D. A. Hawkins
Pte. R. L. Heal
Pte. V. Hebert
Pte. P. Heckman
Cpl. V. E. Heighton
Pte. F. Hepp
Pte. D. N. Hertzberger
Pte. W. H. Hetherington
L./Cpl. W. J. Hewer
Pte. A. E. Hill
Pte. J. G. Hill
L./Cpl. A. Hind
Pte. E. H. Hinz
Pte. G. F. Hoch
Pte. J. Holmes
Pte. T. Holmes
Pte. T. E. Hood
Pte. G. P. Hopf
Pte. R. J. G. Horne
Pte. H. Howell
Pte. A. Hughes
Cpl. A. G. Hunt
Pte. D. L. Hutchins
Pte. W. Hylands
Sergt. J. H. Ivison
Sergt. W. Ivison
Pte. F. T. Jackson

Cpl. J. D. Jamieson
Pte. M. Janzen
Pte. F. A. Jarvo
Pte. T. A. Jeffries
Pte. G. J. Jelso
Pte. H. E. Jepsen
Pte. L. E. Johnson
Pte. I. Q. Jones
Pte. C. A. Joyes
Pte. H. R. Kalbfleisch
Pte. W. J. Kay
Pte. C. H. Kearney
Pte. J. G. Kearney
Pte. R. L. Kearns
Pte. G. H. Kennedy
Pte. W. D. Kennedy
Pte. J. Kerr
Pte. J. H. King
Pte. E. T. Kitching
Pte. H. Knapp
Pte. R. A. J. Knight
Pte. L. Knister
Pte. J. J. Koralewich
Pte. A. Koskovich
Pte. P. Krywiarchuk
Pte. M. Kurkowsky
Pte. P. J. Lacey
Pte. R. Laframboise
Pte. L. A. Langille
Cpl. G. Larkin
Pte. W. J. Larsh
L./Cpl. L. A. Lauzon
Pte. G. Lavallee
Pte. J. V. Lawrence
L./Cpl. J. E. Leclair
Pte. G. W. Leek
Sergt. A. Lennox
Pte. G. H. Leopold
Pte. W. Lies
Pte. J. M. Light
Cpl. C. R. Little
Cpl. F. E. Little
L./Sgt. M. Litvinchuk
Pte. L. G. Lotz
Pte. J. J. Lovell
Sergt. D. A. Lovett
Pte. F. J. Lundquist
Pte. E. I. Lynch
Pte. J. A. Lynde
Pte. N. D. Lyon
Pte. D. S. Lyttle
Pte. A. W. Macdonald
Cpl. H. A. Macdonald
Pte. L. K. Macdonald
Pte. G. S. Macdonell
Pte. J. F. MacLeod
Sergt. W. Macmillan
Pte. W. M. Majury
Pte. H. E. Malott
Pte. G. G. Marr
L./Cpl. N. Marentette
Pte. D. L. Marion
Pte. T. C. Marshall
Pte. H. E. Martin
Pte. W. G. Martin
Pte. W. F. C. Martin

Pte. J. E. Marvyn
Pte. I. F. Matheson
Pte. R. K. Matlock
Pte. F. E. Matte
Pte. R. I. McCarthy
Pte. P. J. McCarty
Pte. M. L. McColl
Pte. K. G. McCombs
Pte. E. R. McCormick
Pte. E. G. McCorry
Pte. B. L. McFadden
L./Cpl. T. L. McGregor
Pte. A. McHugh
L./Cpl. D. H. McIntee
Pte. R. A. McIntosh
Pte. E. F. McIntyre
Pte. R. A. McIntyre
Pte. C. D. McIsaac
Pte. P. H. McKeon
Pte. J. P. McLagan
Pte. F. McLean
Pte. H. R. McLennan
Pte. G. M. McLeod
Pte. C. R. McNutt
Sergt. E. N. Mellott
Pte. G. H. Meroniuk
L./Cpl. D. M. Middleton
L./Cpl. H. M. Millard
Pte. R. C. Miller
Cpl. R. L. Miller
L./Cpl. H. O. Milligan
Pte. B. Mitchell
L./Cpl. F. J. Mitchell
Pte. S. Z. Molnar
Pte. P. J. Morency
Pte. E. J. Morgan
Cpl. P. B. J. Morgan
Pte. C. L. Morley
Pte. A. Morock
Pte. K. A. Morris
Pte. N. R. Morrison
Pte. R. H. Morrison
L./Cpl. A. T. Morton
Pte. L. C. Mowry
Cpl. E. W. Mulholland
Pte. B. W. Murdoch
Pte. R. D. Murphy
Pte. E. A. Neale
Pte. W. J. Needham
Pte. P. A. Nelson
Pte. G. J. Neville
Pte. G. L. Neyrinck
Cpl. G. W. Nicoll
Pte. J. J. O'Brien
Pte. D. O'Connor
Pte. R. L. O'Connor
Pte. J. A. Oldman
Pte. C. O'Neill
Pte. C. J. O'Reilly
Pte. H. F. Painter
Pte. R. Paquette
Pte. E. Parent
Pte. R. J. Parent
Pte. R. Parent
Pte. R. Parliament
Pte. J. D. Pate

L./Cpl. G. E. Patterson
Pte. T. P. Patton
Pte. A. H. Peltier
Pte. L. J. Pierce
Pte. W. D. Pinch
Pte. R. Podger
Pte. L. J. Pollock
Pte. D. Pollon
Pte. W. C. Poole
Pte. C. E. Post
Pte. W. S. Powers
Pte. C. Prouse
Pte. J. T. Pullan
Pte. L. R. Quaife
L./Sgt. N. P. Rawlings
Pte. R. E. Rayner
L./Cpl. C. H. Reid
Pte. L. Reider
Pte. I. N. P. Renaud
Pte. J. Rennie
Pte. L. J. Rice
Pte. V. Riedl
Pte. D. C. Rinker
Pte. A. C. Rivait
Sergt. E. E. Rivait
Pte. L. Rivait
Pte. L. M. Rivait
Pte. R. C. Robinet
L./Cpl. S. H. Roseman
Pte. A. K. Ross
Pte. F. Rowley
Pte. D. F. Royan
Pte. E. S. Royce
Cpl. G. Ryan
Pte. R. H. Sallows
Pte. R. E. Sands
Pte. C. O. Sauer
Pte. G. A. Sauve
Pte. J. Schofield
L./Cpl. C. M. Schooley
Pte. A. F. Schumilas
Pte. E. F. Schweitzer
Cpl. H. E. Scott
Pte. C. J. Searle
Pte. M. Senchuk
Pte. S. Shannon
Pte. D. Shantz
Pte. I. Shawanda
Pte. G. T. Schearer
Pte. F. H. Sheff
Pte. S. P. P. Shepley
Pte. L. L. Shoup
Cpl. J. Shura
Pte. H. Siverns
Pte. F. A. Skead
Pte. T. Skidmore
Cpl. S. Smead
Pte. D. R. Smith
Pte. G. H. Smith
Pte. R. R. Soble
Pte. B. A. Soloway
Cpl. H. J. Sponder
Pte. L. F. Spotton
Pte. H. G. Squire
Pte. J. St. Dennis
Pte. M. St. Louis

Pte. T. Stainton
Pte. R. Stake
Cpl. W. J. Stanley
Pte. E. C. Stanton
Cpl. S. R. Staton
Pte. J. W. Steers
Pte. J. H. Stevens
Pte. G. R. Stevenson
Pte. G. E. Stewart
Pte. S. Stewart
Pte. R. L. Stockdale
Pte. A. W. Storrey
Pte. D. L. Sullivan
Pte. J. L. Sullivan
Pte. W. D. Tasker
L./Cpl. A. J. Taylor
Pte. J. Taylor
Sergt. W. G. Taylor
Pte. J. J. Thibeault
Pte. H. F. Thomas
Sergt. J. L. Thompson
Pte. L. Thompson
Pte. T. Thompson
Pte. C. Thurston
Pte. B. Toman
L./Cpl. R. K. Tomlinson
Pte. E. A. Toombs
Pte. R. K. Towle
L./Cpl. L. J. Trombley
Pte. E. J. Trudell
Pte. A. Tweyman
Pte. W. J. Twining
Pte. D. Vallance
Pte. E. R. Vaughan
Pte. E. Vautour
Pte. B. L. Veinot
Pte. E. A. Walker
Pte. W. F. Walker
Pte. J. Walmsley
Pte. C. R. Ward
Pte. J. A. Watson
Pte. A. A. Webb
Pte. J. A. Weir
Cpl. O. J. West
Pte. H. J. Westfall
Sergt. E. C. S. Wheeler
Pte. E. A. Wheeler
Pte. D. White
Pte. D. R. White
Pte. F. White
Pte. S. M. Whitehead
Pte. R. Wigle
Pte. H. J. Williams
L./Cpl. R. K. Williamson
Sergt. C. R. Wilson
Pte. H. A. Wilson
Pte. K. E. Wilson
Cpl. O. T. Wilson
Pte. W. W. Wilson
Pte. J. H. Wingfield
Pte. W. Winterbottom
Pte. S. Worsley
L./Cpl. M. M. Wright
Pte. V. Wysuki
Pte. W. M. Younger

DECORATIONS

VICTORIA CROSS

Major F. A. Tilston

DISTINGUISHED SERVICE ORDER

Lieut.-Colonel F. K. Jasperson, E.D.
Major K. W. MacIntyre
Major D. W. McIntyre
Lieut.-Colonel J. D. Mingay, M.B.E.
Lieut.-Colonel J. E. C. Pangman, E.D.

OFFICER OF THE ORDER OF THE BRITISH EMPIRE

Lieut.-Colonel P. W. Bennett
Lieut.-Colonel L. A. Deziel
Lieut.-Colonel B. J. S. Macdonald, E.D.
Lieut.-Colonel L. R. McDonald
Colonel A. S. Pearson, E.D.

MEMBER OF THE ORDER OF THE BRITISH EMPIRE

Captain E. L. Cohen
Honorary Major M. J. Dalton
Major J. D. Macfarlane
Major D. Mackenzie
Major J. D. Mingay
Major R. F. Sheppard, M.C., E.D.

W.O.2 (C.S.M.) J. F. Garswood
W.O.1 (R.S.M.) W. J. Lescombe
R.S.M. W. E. Potts
R.S.M. D. F. Wilkinson

MILITARY CROSS

Honorary Captain J. Cardy
Captain P. A. Cropp
Lieut. E. P. Fisher
Lieut. C. D. Gatton
Major A. J. Hodges
Captain J. R. Huff
Lieutenant C. L. Kadey
Captain H. J. Kennedy
Captain D. F. MacRae (attached)
Captain C. A. Richardson
Major T. E. Steele
Lieutenant H. R. Tucker

BRITISH EMPIRE MEDAL

Sergt. J. T. Coughlin

DISTINGUISHED CONDUCT MEDAL

Sergt. S. B. Kirkland
Pte. J. Maier
C.S.M. C. Stapleton

MILITARY MEDAL

Pte. R. A. M. Baker
Pte. W. E. Bradley
Cpl. G. Bruce
Cpl. R. Carle
Pte. L. D. De Laurier
L./Sergt. F. L. Dixon
C.S.M. W. J. Foster
Pte. L. P. Head
Sergt. W. E. Hussey
Pte. G. E. Marchant
Pte. J. H. Mizon
Cpl. W. H. Moriarity
Pte. L. G. Norton
Sergt. H. L. O'Rourke
Sergt. T. W. Ryan

BAR TO MILITARY MEDAL

C.S.M. F. L. Dixon

SECOND BAR TO MILITARY MEDAL

C.S.M. F. L. Dixon

MENTIONED IN DESPATCHES

Captain I. H. Ashbury
Major J. W. Burgess
Honorary Captain J. Cardy
Lieut.-Colonel L. A. Deziel
Lieutenant A. D. Green (killed in action)
Captain A. M. Hayes
Major T. E. Hayhurst, E.D. (killed in action)
Captain F. J. J. Lynch
Major H. J. Kennedy
Captain J. R. Kent
Major S. B. McDonald
Capt. W. L. McGregor
Major D. W. McIntyre
Captain R. W. Meanwell
Captain E. H. Musgrave
Lieutenant J. C. Palms (killed in action)
Lieutenant J. A. Prince
Captain W. H. Scott
Major T. E. Steele
Captain J. R. Turnbull
Captain J. F. S. Walmsley
Lieutenant N. M. Watson
Major J. A. Willis (killed in action)
Captain R. A. Wright

Sergt. F. L. Bennett
Cpl. J. P. Boland (killed in action)
Pte. G. R. Borthwick (killed in action)
Pte. G. D. Brown
Sergt. R. E. A. Burdick (killed in action)

DECORATIONS—continued

Sergt. J. B. Campbell
Pte. S. Carley
Pte. E. R. Cousineau
Pte. J. E. Crockett
Pte. G. C. Deschaine (died of wounds)
Cpl. J. Donaldson
Pte. R. W. Ferrari
C.S.M. W. J. Foster
Pte. F. W. Gehl (killed in action)
Pte. M. G. Hutchison
Cpl. C. H. Jolly
Cpl. R. M. Jones
Cpl. A. E. Kain
Sergt. E. H. Levitt
Sergt. D. A. Lovett (died of wounds)
C.S.M. G. W. Lucas
Cpl. E. N. Mellott
Pte. A. F. A. Montroy
Cpl. C. E. Wendover
L./Cpl. M. M. Wright (killed in action)

COMMANDER-IN-CHIEF'S CERTIFICATE FOR GALLANTRY AND GOOD SERVICE

Pte. W. C. Anderson
Pte. G. R. Borthwick (killed in action)
Pte. J. L. Cassidy
Sergt. D. R. Elvy
L./Cpl. R. J. Heath
Pte. B. L. Jamieson
Pte. A. E. Kain
Pte. P. Markowsky
Pte. I. F. Matheson (killed in action)
Pte. J. H. Moutray
L./Cpl. W. L. Wells

SILVER STAR (U.S.A.)

Major F. J. Chauvin

CROIX DE GUERRE (SILVER STAR)

C.S.M. J. Donaldson

CROIX DE GUERRE (BRONZE STAR)

Pte. S. Carley
Sergt. L. E. Scobie
Sergt. C. C. Wold

BRONZE LION (NETHERLANDS)

Captain C. J. Jeffrey
Lieutenant E. R. Thompson
Captain R. A. Wright

Sergt. J. E. Browell
Sergt. E. H. Levitt

BRONZE CROSS (NETHERLANDS)

C.Q.M.S. L. A. Belland
Sergt. G. P. Campbell
Sergt. L. A. Nahmabin

An example of the Padre's 'next of kin' letter.

Dear Mrs Dunne,

The joy of living a dutiful life is enhanced by the sadness of life, because the example of a dutiful life pierces through the dark clouds to form a silver lining. Who lives a more dutiful life for God and Canada than a soldier in a just war?

"Greater love no man has than a man who lay down his life for his friends". The Holy father Pius XII assures us that he who is struck off in strength with a proper intention in a holy crusade for the cause of freedom and Christianity, has already had his reward, which is nothing less than a martyr's crown, for all eternity.

I have talked to hundreds of the flower of Canada's gallant manhood on active service. Neither the fear of sudden death, nor the thought of long endurance has dismayed them. There is only one explanation. The expression of the Holy Spirit has strengthened their back for the burden, and buoyed up their spirits.

The wives of such noble heroes will never appreciate that they are privileged wives until they meditate on these things. The soldier's life is a vocation, the same as a priest's life is a vocation. The soldier's wife is a sharer in that vocation. She too is a soldier in spirit. It is also fitting and proper that this should be, for she too endures an "unnatural separation". Both will receive their reward.

Such a vocation had William H. Such a vocation has Sarah Lenore. Ah! But your soldier was especially privileged. Fifteen R.C. Canadian soldiers had already been summoned before a priest could arrive. Not so with William. An English Chaplain administered the Last Rites of the Church while William was fully conscious.

I offered the funeral Mass and officiated at beautiful Brookwood Cemetery, where he was gently and reverently laid with full military honors, beside his comrades of this and other battles.

As the bugler sounded the "Last Post", and while dozens of his fellow soldiers held the salute, I felt it was Gabriel's trumpet summoning William the soldier to eternal peace with God. Then on the wings of fancy, my thoughts were with you in far away British Columbia. Sometimes it is harder to live than to die. Tomorrow I shall offer my Mass for you and your children.

"as I lean upon my Barracks altar stairs
Which through the Black-out slopes to God".

We shall keep the memory green in a well cared plot of one who lies in honored glory. It is for you, as well as for us to dedicate our lives, to guard the principles for which he was impatient to fight for, to defend.

If he had something to die for, you have something to live for. Please recite the enclosed "Prayer of a Soldier in France" (by Joyce Kilmer). Do this in memory of a husband and father, for the Canadian Army overseas.

Soldier Wife, you still have duty to God and Country and your family. We who are about to close in the ranks to "carry on", salute you from the front lines of Freedom.

God Bless you all
Padre M.J.Dalton

Rev. Major Mike Dalton's War Medals

Medal descriptions left to right

Member of the Order of the British Empire.
The 1939–45 Star: minimum 6 months overseas between Sept.3,1939 and Sept.2,1945.
The France and Germany Star: participation in operational service between Jun.6,1944 and May 8,1945 for the invasion of France, Belgium, Holland, or Germany.
The Defence Medal: minimum of six months service military or civilian, subject to air attack or otherwise closely threatened.
The Canadian Volunteer Service Medal: 18 months voluntary service in Canadian forces between Sept.3,1939 and Mar.1,1947.
The War Medal: minimum 28 days in armed services from Sept.3,1939 to Sept.2,1945.

Member of the Order of the British Empire.

The medal was created by King George V in 1917 to honor men and women who were non combatants. It was awarded for service as well as gallantry.

Father Mike was one of the first Catholic Canadian Chaplains to be awarded this prestigious honor.
It was presented to him by King George VI on June 2 1943. Although it seems like something in line with his character, Mike did not, as has been reported, reach into his pocket and give the King a religious medal. To correct another erroneous report, a record of medals given to members of the Essex Scottish, verifies that Father Mike did not, as reported, receive a Military Cross Medal.

George R.I.

George the Sixth

by the Grace of God of Great Britain, Ireland and the British Dominions beyond the Seas, King, Defender of the Faith, Emperor of India and Sovereign of the Most Excellent Order of the British Empire to Our trusty and well beloved Michael Joseph Morgan Dalton Esquire Honorary Captain active Honorary Major in the Military Forces of Our Dominion of Canada

Greeting

Whereas We have thought fit to nominate and appoint you to be an Additional Member of the Military Division of Our said Most Excellent Order of the British Empire We do by these presents grant unto you the Dignity of an Additional Member of Our said Order and hereby authorise you to have hold and enjoy the said Dignity and Rank of an Additional Member of Our aforesaid Order together with all and singular the privileges thereunto belonging or appertaining.

Given at Our Court at Saint James's under Our Sign Manual and the Seal of Our said Order this Second day of June 1943 in the Seventh year of Our Reign

By the Sovereign's Command

Mary R
Grand Master

Grant of the dignity of an Additional Member of the Military Division of the Order of the British Empire to Honorary Captain (active Honorary Major) Michael Joseph Morgan Dalton.

Military Abbreviations

Capt.	Captain	Fd.Amb.	Field Ambulance
Rev.	Reverend	B.O.R.	Battalion Orderly Room.
H.M.S.	Her majesty's Ship		
V.C.	Victoria Cross	Y.M.C.A.	Young Men's Christian Association
M.C.	Military Cross		
R.H.L.I.	Royal Hamilton Light Infantry	T.L.C.	Tank Landing Craft
		M.O.	Medical Officer
R.Reg.C. (R.C.R.)	Royal Regiment of Canada	M.B.E.	Member of the Order of the British Empire
A.A.	Anti Aircraft	C.B.E.	Commander of the British Empire
H.Q.	Headquarters		
O.C.Col.	Commanding Officer Colonel	A.T.S.	Auxillary Territorial Service
C.Co.	'C' Company	Pte.	Private
R.C.E.	Royal Canadian Engineers	F.D.S.	Field Dressing Station
		R.C.A.S.C.	Royal Canadian Army Service Corps
R.A.F	Royal Air force		
M.C.L.	Military Craft Landing	C.M.H.Q.	Canadian Military Headquarters
Bde.	Brigade		
A.L.C.	Amphibious Landing Craft	Inf. Bde.	Infantry Brigade
		C.P.C.	Canadian Postal Corps
B.H.Q.	Brigade Headquarters	Div.	Division
M.D.S.	Medical Dressing Station	B.E.F.	British Expeditionary Force
R.C.	Roman Catholic	D.S.O.	Distinguished Service Order
R.I.P.	Rest in Peace		
R.R.C. (R.C.R.)	Royal Regiment of Canada	R.C.A.F.	Royal Canadian Air Force
G.H.	General Hospital	V.1.	Vergelfungswaffe (Flying Bomb)
R.C.A.	Royal Canadian Artillery		
		V.E.Day	Victory in Europe
O.C.	Officer Commanding	C.W.A.C.	Canadian Women's Army Corps
Recce.	Reconnaissance		
O.C.Lt.Co.	Officer Commanding Lieutenant Colonel	Q.M.G.	Quartermaster General
		A.R.C.	American Red Cross
O.B.E.	Member of the Order of the British Empire	M.M.	Military Medal
Can.G.H.	Canadian General Hospital		

149

Bibliography

Captain, Adj. R.W. Meanwell (ed)
1st Battalion The Essex Scottish
Regiment 1939- 1945
Gale and Polden 1946

Col. C.P. Stacey
The Official History of
the Canadian Army
in the Second World War
Vol.1 Six Years of War
Vol.2 The Canadians in Italy
Vol.3 The Victory Campaign
Queens Printer 1967

Terry Copp & Bill McAndrew
Battle Exhaustion
Soldiers and Psychiatrists in the
Canadian Army 1939- 1945
McGill-Queens University Press

Gwynne Dyer
War
Crown Publishers

Barry Broadfoot
The Veterans' Years
Coming Home from the War
Douglas and McIntyre

Horley   Aug 21 1942

1800 hrs to av 14 B.H - many wounded

Brought cigarettes, beads etc
to wounded.
Eve - notified all Regiments
R.C.A   & 8th Recce of
times of Sunday masses
9.30 home for supper. Col
Mothersill new O.C.

The tragedy of Dieppe
only one Essex officer returned
& he was attached from Glengarry
Regt. Out of 30 officers who
lived together at aldershot &
previously I am the only
original others had been
transferred or shot down in France
Remnant of once proud &
gallant outfit are quiet,
solemn, but morale is high.
Lads say they are glad I didn't go
I couldn't have done much
good - In plan of United actions,
Dieppe was no tragedy but blessing